THE HOLMAN GUIDE
TO
INTERPRETING
THE BIBLE

DAVID S. DOCKERY AND GEORGE H. GUTHRIE

**BROADMAN
& HOLMAN
PUBLISHERS**

Nashville, Tennessee

The Holman Guide to Interpreting the Bible
Copyright © 2004 by Broadman & Holman Publishers

ISBN 978-0-8054-2858-2

Dewey Decimal Classification: 220.6
Subject Heading: BIBLE—CRITICISM, INTERPRETATION, ETC.

Printed in the USA

3 4 5 6 7 8 9 10 • 12 11 10 09 08 07

CONTENTS

CHAPTER ONE

THE IMPORTANCE OF BIBLICAL INTERPRETATION

The story is told of a lady who went to catch a flight at the airport. She was in a hurry and had not had time to eat, so on the way to her gate she stopped at a newsstand to pick up a pack of cookies. When she arrived at the gate she found a seat, and in the seat next to her, just on the other side of a little table, sat an older gentleman. After a few minutes, and to her shock, the man picked up the pack of cookies from the table, opened it, and, with a smile, popped a cookie in his mouth. He placed the cookies back on the table and munched away happily. She was shocked and stunned for a moment! Nevertheless, not wanting to make a scene, the lady picked up the pack of cookies, took one out, and too began eating. She then placed the pack back on the table, thinking the man would not have the audacity to repeat his offense. Yet, he did. Again he took a cookie, looked at it thoughtfully, nibbled, and then gobbled the rest down. Now she was seething inside. How dare he help himself to her cookies! Still fuming, the lady took another cookie from its wrapper and popped it in her mouth. Now there was just one cookie left. To add insult to injury, the gentleman took the last cookie, broke it in half, slid one half to her, and ate the remaining half. Then, with a smile and a nod, the gentleman got up and left. Boy, was she mad! Thankfully, her flight number was called and passengers were asked to board. Mumbling to herself about the selfishness of some people, she got up and made her way to the gate. On the way to the gate the lady reached into her purse to get out her boarding pass and there found *her pack of cookies!*

How embarrassing! The lady traveler was so caught up in the hurry and hunger of the moment, she did not even know whose cookies were at stake! I am sure we all can identify with losing perspective in the rush and crush of life, and one of the areas that tends to get out of focus is our intake of God's Word. In Mark 4:18-19 Jesus interprets the seed that fell on thorny ground as the Word falling into a life that has lost an eternal perspective. The cares of life, the lure of wealth, and the desire for nice things, Jesus tells us, can choke the Word out of a person's life, just as weeds choke the life out of a would-be productive plant.

Others are sown among thorns; these are the ones who hear the word, but the worries of this age, the pleasure of wealth, and the desires for other things enter in and choke the word, and it becomes unfruitful.—Mark 4:18-19, HCSB

You probably are interested in God's Word and in being used in God's work, or you would not have this book in your hands right now. Yet, you may be at a place in life where you need to regain perspective—to remember how important Bible study and the good work of interpretation are for a healthy Christian life and ministry. So, let's move our hearts away from those other "cookies" that tend to be so distracting—those "weeds" that crowd out our hunger for the Scriptures—and think in a fresh way about why Bible study, coupled with sound interpretation, is so important. There are three very important reasons, and they all revolve around why God created us in the first place. The reason *why* you exist has everything to do with *why* you should take biblical interpretation very seriously.

In my home are a wide variety of tools. My wife has tools in the kitchen, some very expensive, but most very simple and economical. For instance she has a mixer and a gas cooktop (examples of the expensive items), as well as an egg separator and a "tea ball" (examples of the inexpensive items). On my tools shelf you can find a screwdriver, a nail set, and a tape measure, for instance, and out in the

shop you might stumble on my handy
Makita circular saw. My tools also vary in
price as well as their functions. When my
wife reaches for a tool in the kitchen, or I seek
out a tool for some project, there are two issues
that are paramount at that moment: (1) the tool's availability and (2)
the tool's ability to fulfill the purpose for which it was created. The
most inexpensive tool is a most valuable tool when it functions as its
creator intended to meet the need of the moment.

You may not feel very fancy as a Christian or very gifted as a minister. You may feel like a tool that has been misplaced or fashioned
out of inferior materials. Yet, God purchased you with a great price
(Rv 5:9; 14:4), and has very specific purposes for you *in relation to
himself, in your fulfillment as a person*, and *in your ministry to others*.
The key is your availability to him for the fulfilling of those purposes, and that availability has much to do with your intake of God's
Word. Let's take a look at how hearing God's Word rightly interpreted has an impact on your relationship with God, your own joy in life,
and your ministry to others.

TO KNOW GOD

First of all, *you were created to know God in an intimate relationship.* We see this throughout the Scriptures, beginning with creation,
through the covenants that culminate with the cross, and all the way
to the coming of Christ at the end of the age. We as human beings, in
our first parents Adam and Eve, fell away from God. Abraham
received the promise and covenant with
God that established a special relationship
with God and would issue forth in a nation
to bless all nations. That nation, the
Israelites, later agreed to and then rebelled
against God's gracious offer of a covenant
relationship at Sinai. Throughout the Old
Testament, God constantly calls out for his

"God does not ask
your ability or your
inability. He asks
only your availability."

Mary Kay Ash

7

people to "hear," to "call" to him, to "seek" him, and to "thirst for" him. Relationship obviously is very important to God. Yet, nowhere can the importance of relationship be seen with greater clarity than in the promise of a new covenant (Jr 31:31-34) and in its fulfillment in Jesus' death and resurrection. God paid a great price to establish a new covenant relationship with us. That relationship will find its ultimate fulfillment when Christ takes us, as his bride, to the great wedding feast at the end of the age. It is all about relationship.

> *"Listen! I stand at the door and knock. If anyone hears My voice and opens the door, I will come in to him and have dinner with him, and he with Me."—Jesus (Rv 3:20)*

There are at least three ways the Scriptures, as rightly interpreted, have a profound effect on us fulfilling our purpose (that is, of God fulfilling it in us) of knowing God. First, *God chose to communicate with human beings through human language.* John Calvin wrote that God, in giving us the Scriptures, has accommodated himself to human language. This means that God chose human words, issued by real human beings, at real places in the world, at real times in history, to communicate with us as the human race. Receiving those words as God's messages to us, hearing accurately what God intended to communicate, forms the basis for how God speaks to us. In other words,

"Just as old or bleary-eyed men and those with weak vision, if you thrust before them a most beautiful volume, even if they recognize it to be some sort of writing, yet can scarcely construe two words, but with the aid of spectacles will begin to read distinctly; so Scripture , gathering up the otherwise confused knowledge of God in our minds, having dispersed our dullness, clearly shows us the true God."

John Calvin
Institutes of the Christian Religion, I,vi, 1

if we do not hear God's Word accurately, we have no basis for relationship with God in the first place. General revelation, God's revelation of himself through nature and history, can form a backdrop, but we as humans hear God's voice give *specific* messages concerning his will and ways through his Word, the Bible, as it is rightly interpreted.

"Lord Jesus Christ, open the eyes of my heart... illumine my eyes with your light – you alone, the only light."

John Chrysotom's prayer before reading Scripture

This brings us to a second reason Bible interpretation is so important for our relationship with God: *God has chosen his Word as a means of communicating his invitation to relationship, the gospel.* In Romans 10:14-15 Paul writes,

But how, then, can they call on Him in whom they have not believed in? And how can they believe without hearing about Him? And how can they hear without a preacher? And how can they preach unless they are sent? As it is written, "How welcome are the feet of those who announce the gospel of good things!"

Faith in Christ comes by hearing the Word of God. The mystery of salvation, in part, is that God effects in human hearts a supernatural, eternal work of spiritual deliverance and transformation by using his divine Word rightly spoken by human lips. God's Word must be rightly interpreted because the gospel must be heard clearly.

Third, *God has called us to hear his Word as a means of growing in our relationship with him.* In 1 Peter 2:2 Peter challenges us, "Like newborn infants, desire the unadulterated spiritual milk, so that you may grow by it in [your] salvation, since you have tasted that the Lord is good." The images of milk and meat were used broadly in the ancient world to distinguish elementary from advanced teachings. However, wherever a person is on the spiritual maturity scale, it is the Word of God that the biblical writers point to as the means of spiritual nourishment and growth. You and I must have a steady intake of

God's Word if we are to experience spiritual maturity and, thus, ever deepening relationship with our Lord. This brings us to a second reason we should want to interpret the Bible responsibly.

EXPERIENCING A FULFILLING LIFE

Several commentators on Christian culture at the dawn of the twenty-first century rightly have pointed out that the modern church too often focuses on human fulfillment to the exclusion of the more weighty teachings of Christian doctrine. They are concerned that moderns are fed a sugary substitute for God's Word, a diet both self-focused and devoid of real spiritual nourishment. This concern is a real one and one to which we will return shortly. However, there is what John Piper calls a biblical "Christian hedonism," that suggests human fulfillment is a topic widely addressed in the Bible. The Scriptures proclaim that people should seek fulfillment, and that fulfillment is found as we abandon our own agendas to God's agendas for us. God wants us to have fullness of life, the abundant life Christ came to bring. We are invited to experience that abundant, joy-filled life had by those who follow God's Word, and nowhere do we see this more clearly than in Psalm 119. Notice some of the benefits experienced by those who follow God's Word as witnessed by this incredible psalm. Do you want to know a source of true happiness in life? See verses 1, 2, 35, 56. How about pleasure? See verse 103. Do you need strengthening in the area of integrity, or do you lack stability, or endurance? See verses 1, 3, 89-92, 133, or 140. Perhaps you need wisdom or guidance in the face of a difficult decision and should look to verses 19, 24, 98, 100, 105, or 133 for the source of those gifts. On the other hand you may be running low on emotional resources and should look to verse 28 for the source

> "...the sweet joy with which the hidden mouth of his heart partook of Thy Bread, I had no inkling or experience."
>
> Augustine on remembering Bishop Ambrose's love of Scripture

of encouragement, verses 25, 40, or 83 for emotional and physical renewal, or verse 143 for the key to joy while under pressure or stress. Verses 18, 34, 66, 142, 151, 160, and 165 extend an offer to know truth, have knowledge, and learn obedience through the Word. Difficulties and times of trial go with life, and so you may be needing hope, freedom, deliverance, a way to avoid disgrace, or comfort. That the Word of God is the means to all of these may be found in verses 6, 31, 43, 45, 49, 50, 81, and 114. In short the Word of God addresses and offers help in almost any circumstance in which we could find ourselves. It promises joy, fulfillment, help, and hope for those who will take it seriously. Ironically, to value God's Word above our own agendas is to find the source for experiencing life in its fullness.

The story is told of a rich old man whose son had died tragically many years before he himself passed. Since he had no remaining family, his incredible wealth, including numerous valuable paintings, statues, and artifacts, was to be auctioned, and the event was greatly anticipated as art dealers and collectors dreamed of obtaining pieces of the old man's lifelong love of precious artwork. The day came for the auction, and the first item on the block surprised everyone. Rather than one of the more valuable pieces, the auctioneer brought forward a rather simple portrait of the old man's son. Those present could see it had little value, and, consequently, the only person to bid on it was an old butler who had known and cared for the boy. When the auctioneer had closed the bidding for the portrait, he looked at the butler and took a note out of his pocket. He announced that he had been instructed to read this note after the first portrait had sold. In the note, the old man proclaimed his desire that his entire fortune be given to whoever bought the picture of his son. The butler, by valuing what the old man had valued above all his possessions, had unwittingly opened a door to unimaginable wealth.

By analogy, God has placed incredible significance on his Word. In essence, the invitation of Psalm 119 is to value what God values above what we would value, given our natural inclinations. In valuing the Word above the words of our culture, or friends, or self, we open a door to unimaginable spiritual wealth and find real joy—the joy that God has intended for people from the very beginning. This is not a smiley-face version of the faith. The Bible still deals openly and honestly with the hard side of life. Sometimes obedience leads to joy through incredible suffering (Heb 12:1-2). Yet, the longing for happiness and joy in life, the desire for peace and comfort, stability and significance, are God-given longings and only found in a life open to him through his Word. This desire for significance, in part, we find fulfilled as God uses us in ministry to others, which brings us to the final way Bible interpretation helps us fulfill God's purposes for us.

MINISTRY TO OTHERS

We have said that a biblical approach to finding fulfillment in life involves feasting on God's Word. The product of such fulfillment will be a focus on the needs of others and the addressing of those needs in ministry. On the other hand, a fleshly form of seeking self-fulfillment can be recognized by its focus on self as the end-all goal. We were created to know God and to bring him glory by receiving his fullness of life through his Word, but we were also created to glorify God and advance his causes in this world through ministry to others. At the heart of that ministry, rightly executed, stands the Word of God and our appropriate handling of it.

Interpretation of the Bible has a powerful impact on others—whether that interpretation is good or bad, used properly or abused. Proper interpretation of the Bible has changed lives, set in motion revivals, transformed nations, and given hope to countless millions. Yet, poor interpretation, on the other hand, has fostered heresies, given lunatics a tool of abuse, destroyed families, and eaten the heart out of churches. Interpretation, even very bad interpretation, is quite potent, and, therefore, deserves serious consideration. With right interpretation we can be used to advance God's kingdom. If, however, we are given to faulty interpretation, we can do great damage to our own spiritual lives and the lives of others. Thus, there are at least four reasons we need to interpret the Scriptures well so that we can minister well to others.

CONFUSING OUR WORDS
WITH GOD'S

First of all, *it is possible to confuse our words with God's words.* After all, we are so used to hearing ourselves talk, so used to hearing the phrases and philosophies that surround our lives, that we can continue to hear them even as we think we are hearing God's Word speak to us. Gordon Fee and Douglas Stuart tell of a lady who went to her pastor and announced God had told her to divorce her husband. When asked what she meant, she said that she had read Paul's encouragement to "put off the old man"! Now the phrase "old man," when used to speak of one's husband, is a distinctly modern, American expression. Paul never would have intended his statement to be used as a validation of divorce. In this case, the words from American culture were confused with the Word of God.

In reality we all interpret the Bible every time we pick it up. The question is whether we are interpreting it accurately. Are we seeing what God intended or merely looking at our own reflections smiling back at us? Are we getting past our presuppositions to what God meant to convey through the text? Some expressions of the philosophy called Postmodernism, a pervasive influence on modern Western culture, suggest that all interpretations are equally valid. The picture of people sitting around a Sunday School class or a Bible study group and all arriving at different interpretations of a passage would be applauded as enlightened and an appropriate aim of "interpretation." Yet, this view, when pushed a bit further, has serious flaws. Should everyone's interpretation be seen as valid? Hitler? David Koresh? Really? If in such cases there is "good" interpretation and "bad" interpretation, why not among interpreters who sit around in a friendly discussion group?

> "Readers who treat the text as a mirror onto which they project their own devices and desires fail to distinguish author and reader and so fall prey to interpretive idolatry."
>
> Kevin J. Vanhoozer

The biblical worldview, on the other hand suggests that God has spoken truth through his Word and that people should seek to understand that truth and adjust their understanding to fit God's perspective. Right interpretation means to bring one's interpretation in line with God's intended meaning as given in a place and at a time of history.

The stakes are highest, it seems, for those who wish to be teachers of the Word. James 3:1 states, "Not many should become teachers, my brothers, knowing that we will receive a stricter judgment." The idea, of course, is that when as teachers we confuse our words with God's Word, the lives of others are at stake.

"With the current rise and popularity of the cults, false teachings, and non-biblical philosophies, it is imperative that Christians be grounded in the Word of God so that we can discern error from truth."

Rick Warren

In Jeremiah 8:7-8 the Lord proclaims a judgment against religious leaders who twist the Word of God. They were asserting that they were wise because they had the law of the Lord. Yet, God confronts them with their twisting of Scripture: "How can you say, 'We are wise because we have the law of the LORD,' when your teachers have twisted it so badly?" (NLT). In reality God says that their twisting of Scripture is tantamount to *rejecting* God's Word. In other words, what they thought they were embracing they really were pushing away by their own misinterpretation. They were presenting what they thought were the words of God, but in reality what were their own words. What was the consequence? Jeremiah 8:9-12 states such "wise" men are put to shame and brought to severe punishment.

If we preach our own prejudices, our culture's spiritual fancies (be they in "conservative" or "liberal" guise), rather than the Word of God, we have in fact rejected the Word of God for a lesser communication and stand under the judgment of God. Thus, we need to learn the processes of proper interpretation so that we can distinguish between our words and the words of God.

LEADING OTHERS IN THE PURSUIT OF TRUTH

Second, *we need to learn to study the Bible and interpret it well so we can help guide individuals as well as the church in general.* Most pastors and Bible teachers have experienced the "What do I do in this situation?" type of question from those to whom they are ministering. The issue is, what will be the basis for our encouragement to others? When they are seeking wisdom, to what source will we point them? When they are seeking theological answers, how will we field their questions? When they are seeking comfort, will we be able to direct them to a truly helpful source? Will we depend on our wisdom, our insights, our witty or pet answers, or will we be able to lead them in discovering the bedrock truths found in the Bible? Of course there are occasions, such as horrible abuse or addiction, when the wisest course for us, the most effective form of ministry, is to refer a person to a biblically oriented professional who can deal with the person on a deeper level. Yet, in our day-in, day-out ministries, do we counsel people on the basis of biblical truth or on the basis of something else?

A number of years ago I was co-pastor of a local church, and one of the people seeking membership came by for a talk. The theology taught by the church was hanging him up at points because he was raised in a very different tradition. We took our time, working through seven or eight passages relevant to his questions. We talked about the context of the passages and how they fit together in a theological framework. We discussed his understanding of certain truths and compared those to what the text said at points. When we finished he told me that he had never had anyone deal with him in depth in the Scriptures on that issue. Yet, he was ready to adjust his life to the truth.

On another occasion I was teaching a class on the New Testament, and many non-Christians were in the class. One young lady, who probably was in her early thirties, came to my office for counseling, informing me that God was leading her to get an abortion. When asked how she came to that conclusion, she said that she had prayed about it and felt it was the only way for her career to stay on track. We took time to look at the issue of the sanctity of life in the Bible, addressing those passages that suggest that God is interested in human beings even prior to birth. She was receptive and changed her mind about getting an abortion. I was able to put her in touch with a crisis pregnancy center in that city, and they helped her with the challenges she would face in the coming months.

By virtue of our positions, whether we are pastors, Bible study leaders, or lay teachers, people will come our way with sincere questions. We need to be able to direct them to the specifics in God's Word for answers.

When we move this idea to the next level, we suggest that Scripture must be the basis for the workings of any church. What is the basis upon which we as the leaders of local congregations lead the church? Do we and other leaders in our churches have a clear picture of the difference between those things we do that are culturally driven or traditionally driven or power driven as opposed to those that are driven biblically? Let us make clear from the beginning that there is nothing wrong with traditional or cultural elements in the church—we all have them and they can, at times, play important roles in ministry and worship. Traditions offer stability, a sense of history, and familiarity. Cultural elements can be used to make a bridge to non-Christians in the culture. The problem comes, however, when the traditional and cultural begin to take precedence over what is biblical. The worst cases come when the church is thrown into a power struggle, and those who wish to lead are driving church dynamics on the basis of personality, prejudice, or agendas that have nothing to do with a biblical approach to church life.

> *"You revoke God's word by your tradition that you have handed down. And you do many other similar things."*
>
> —*Jesus (Mk 7:13)*

We should from time to time get the leadership of our churches together and evaluate how we are doing in leading the church in a biblical vision of church life. We must know the Scriptures and interpret them well to be able to do this. It means, however, attempting to get back to square one in our thinking and being courageous enough to ask ourselves very hard questions about why we do what we do.

About seven years ago I participated in a church plant in a local Baptist association. We took several months prior to the establishment of a core group to work through what the Bible says the church should be. The only rule was that we could not talk about cultural applications, such as when we would meet, how the services would be arranged, and such, until we had come up with a clear picture of what the church is to be about biblically. It was difficult for all of us to strip away our normal experience of church and look honestly at what the Bible does and does not say about our experiences as a community of faith. When all was said and done our insights focused on three primary areas: the church is to worship God, the church is to reach the lost, and the church is to build itself up through the exercising of spiritual gifts in love. As we looked at worship, the head of the association at that time commented, "You know, we call the Sunday morning service a 'worship service,' but I don't know if true worship goes on much." So we discussed how we could foster the biblical principle of worship in the life of this new church. When we discussed evangelism, we looked at many ways people are reached for Christ in our culture, but we tried to make an important distinction between what are expressly biblical and what are cultural applications of what is biblical.

Whether your church would be described as "traditional" or "contemporary," think for a moment about how you preach or teach, about when you meet for church, about how you dress, what you sing, and about the elements of your services. Think also about meetings conducted in the life of your church, about how you make decisions on the macro- and micro-levels, and how you deal with problems. Stop and consider for a moment that the *form* of all of the above probably would be quite foreign to Jesus and Paul if they suddenly walked in your door. In the same way, if you and I could be transported into a first-century church setting, we would feel terribly out of place in many ways. This does not make our cultural or traditional expres-

> **"For it is not what a church practices, but what it is warranted [authorized] to practice: not what it holds for a truth, but what it is warranted [authorized] to hold as the word of truth. The Word was written after the church; but as it is the Word of God, it is before it."**
>
> John Collins

sions of church wrong—culture is a fact of life, as are traditions. Yet, the key question is this: When you move the next level down to the bottom line of why you do what you do, *are there biblical principles driving your existence?* If not, the lack thereof will have profound implications in the life of your church. Again, we must know the Bible and grapple with interpreting it faithfully in order to lead the church in living out a biblical vision of what it means to be a community of faith.

COMBATING POOR TEACHING AND HERESY

Third, *we must study the Bible well to combat poor teaching and heresy.* In *The Last Battle*, the finale of C. S. Lewis' Chronicles of Narnia series, an evil ape named Shift, who has joined himself to Narnia's enemies, hatches a plan to dupe the inhabitants of that fair country. Aslan, the lion who serves as the Christ figure in the Chronicles, has not been seen in Narnia for years, so the good beasts of the land do not know what he looks like. Shift, upon finding a lion's skin, ties it to the back of a dim-witted donkey named Puzzle and at night brings this fake Aslan out of a stable and into the eerie light of a great campfire. The donkey does not speak—Shift does all the speaking for him—and, having made a brief appearance, is hustled back into the darkness of the stable. Some of the animals are skeptical but are cowed by threats of great punishment from "Aslan," whom Shift makes out to be a horrible tyrant. As time goes, on Shift begins to make references to Tash, the evil god of the Calorman nation, suggesting that he and Aslan really are one and the same. Shift's plot gives him power over good beasts for a time, even though that power is both misappropriated and misused. All is confusion until the real Aslan and children called from our world arrive to set things right. Shift's misinterpretation and misrepresentation of Aslan dissolve before the power and presence of the Real Lion.

From the beginning of time, where there has been truth, there have been attempts at perverting it, and false teaching always hurts the lives of people. Satan, after all, is "the father of lies" who seeks to steal from people and destroy them. Like Shift in *The Last Battle*, Satan's workers are always peddling half-truths and non-truths to whoever will listen. Therefore, we must study the Bible well in order to be able to address poor or false teaching.

In the mid-1980s I was a first-year Ph.D. student in Fort Worth, Texas. One afternoon two young men who were Jehovah's Witnesses came to my door and wanted to talk. After brief introductions I asked them what they believed about Jesus. As they explained their view, that Jesus was not God, one of them, pointing to the Greek text of John 1, said, "The Greek text of John proves that Jesus was just *a* god, not *the* God." I asked them to wait a moment and, going inside, brought back my Greek New Testament and asked them to look at it with me. Using their own materials, they pointed to the use of the Greek word *Theos* in verse 1, noting that there is no article before that term. So, those who had put together their materials translated the verse something like this, "In the beginning was the Word, and the Word was with God, and the Word was *a* god." The lack of an article in Greek

> "Make a mistake in the interpretation of one of Shakespeare's plays, falsely scan a piece of Spenserian verse, and there is unlikely to be an entailment of eternal consequence; but we cannot accept the similar laxity in the interpretation of Scripture. We are dealing with God's thoughts: we are obligated to take the greatest pains to understand them truly and to explain them clearly."
>
> D. A. Carson

19

constituted a key building block for their understanding of Jesus.

Unfortunately, as I pointed out to them, their building block has a severe crack, since it consists of a faulty understanding of Greek grammar. You see, in Greek a word does not have to have an article in front of it for it to be definite, especially when there is only one of something. What the teachers of these Jehovah's Witnesses did not tell them is that the word *Theos* as used in John's Gospel does not have an article in front of it at several points in the book, and often the context is clear that the one, true God is the object of discussion. In fact, just five verses later in John 1:6 John tells us, "There was a man sent from God." No article occurs in front of the term translated "God." Yet, it is clear that God the Father is in view.

However, cults are not the only concern. Poor teaching also hurts lives in dramatic ways. In his book, *The Bible Jesus Used*, Philip Yancey tells about well-meaning but biblically shallow people who, taking the place of Job's accusers, tell the person sick with cancer that God is punishing him or her. The purveyors of the health and wealth gospel mislead millions each year, diverting their spiritual lives into a barely cloaked materialism that has them seeing God's will through gold-colored glasses. I once knew a lady who rejected faith in God because she had a "word from God" that her husband was going to come back to her. He had left her for another woman. When he did not come back, she accused God of lying to her and turned her back on him. Many philosophy spinners of our day suggest that what a person believes really does not matter as long as the person is sincere. Yet, beliefs have vast implications for the lives of individuals and those around them. False ideas hurt lives. Therefore, we need to study the Bible, interpreting it well, so we can teach the truth. Truth matters.

BEARING WITNESS TO THE GOSPEL

Finally, *we must study and interpret well to be able to share the gospel clearly.* It may seem odd at first blush that we would suggest that study and interpretation have something to do with evangelism.

However, if you look at Acts, notice how Peter, Paul, and others tie their sharing of the gospel to interpretations of the older testament. They interpret the text for their hearers, leading them to an understanding of Jesus based on the Scriptures. Another way of thinking about it is this: The more clearly we think about the gospel, the more clearly we will be able to explain it to others.

> **"If private 'revelations' agree with the Scripture, they are needless, and if they disagree, they are false."**
>
> John Owen

Several years ago at Union University a young man, a player on the basketball team, attended my New Testament class. Eric was a good student and a great guy to be around, but it was obvious that much of what we discussed in class was new to him. He was also involved in a social organization at the time, and that organization was made up of many committed Christians, a number of whom were meeting together regularly for Bible study. At the end of the semester Eric came to my office to talk. He explained that through the Bible study and the New Testament class he had come to understand Christianity for the first time. I asked him if he was ready to commit himself to a new covenant relationship with Jesus (we had dealt a lot with the new covenant in class, so I knew he understood the concept well). Eric said he was, and so we prayed together, and that young man has been a committed follower of Christ ever since. Eric is now a coach in our city, and some of my students told me that he recently shared his faith in Christ as he was being interviewed on the radio.

> **"If the real theologians had tackled this laborious work of translation about a hundred years ago, when they began to lose touch with the people (for whom Christ died), there would have been no place for me."**
>
> C. S. Lewis (rejoinder to Dr. Norman Pittenger)

Of course there have been those in my classes who never "got it." There have been others who "got it," in terms of understanding the gospel, but never came to a place of commitment. The point is this: Eric heard clear presentations of the gospel for the first time in his life in a context where people loved him and were willing to help him work through his questions. The interpretation of the gospel in terms of a covenant relationship seemed to help as well.

Too often we fall into the trap of using catch phrases that mean something in our immediate church culture but do not communicate with those outside. On one occasion I was sharing the gospel with a young lady who was Jewish by birth but an atheist by confession. When I used the phrase "relationship with Jesus," I could tell it did not communicate. I asked her why. It dawned on me as we talked that for her, a young single girl, the word "relationship" with a male figure often had sexual overtones. So, I backed up and came at my explanation using other language that she would understand.

One thing our constant study of the Bible will do for us is challenge our clichés. As we deal with texts that deal with evangelism in the New Testament, we should ask ourselves how the truths of those texts come over into our experiences and ministries. Are we studying and thus sharing on a deeper level? When a non-Christian friend asks a sincere question about the Bible, are we prepared either to answer with integrity, because we have thought deeply about the matter, or commit to considering the question more deeply in light of Scripture? Real evangelism benefits from a commitment to study and right interpretation.

CONCLUSION

In this first chapter we have attempted to lay a foundation for what is to come. In essence we have suggested that we should study the Bible and work hard at interpretation because of significant purposes for which God has created us. We should study and learn to study more effectively because such study is a key to a healthy, growing relationship with God, a key to fulfillment as a person, and a key for ministry to others. In relationship with our children, my wife and I have made it a habit to have them come and look us in the eyes when we are instructing them (they are 8 and 11 years of age). We know that they will "hear" us and have a much better chance of following through with the instructions appropriately if they are tuned in to our words, riveting their attention by looking us in the eyes. As we look to God in his Word, taking time to focus intently on his message, we find a home in relation to him, peace as persons, and effectiveness in ministering to others. Bible study and interpretation, therefore, should be central concerns of our lives as Christians.

WHAT IF...

IN THE MIDST OF WRITING HIS EPISTLE TO THE
ROMANS, IT OCCURRED TO PAUL THAT IN THE
FUTURE SOME WOULD INVEST THEIR ENTIRE
CAREERS DISSECTING HIS EVERY WORD AND WHY
HE USED AN ARTICLE HERE AND DIDN'T THERE.
IT UNNERVED HIM SO BADLY HE ALMOST WAS
UNABLE TO FINISH.

CHAPTER TWO

A BRIEF HISTORY OF THE USE AND INTERPRETATION OF THE BIBLE

A student inquired of his professor as to the meaning of a biblical passage. The teacher answered the student: "It means what it says." The inquiring student raised a follow-up question: "But what does it say?" All texts require interpretation, and we have seen the importance of interpreting texts faithfully in our first chapter. Yet, discovering the meaning of biblical texts is not always easy.

Throughout the history of the church there has been disagreement over how to carry out the responsibility of the interpretive task. Before we offer principles for interpretation, it will be helpful to learn from those who have gone before us.

At the heart of these discussions throughout the history of the church have been two paramount questions: (1) How many meanings does a text have? and (2) Where is/are meaning(s) located? Thus, since the beginning of the church, a dual heritage has developed: (1) one maintains that Scripture's meaning is found only in its primary, historical sense and (2) the other considers Scripture's ultimate meaning to rest in its fuller sense.

"When studying biblical interpretation, it is important to bear in mind that there are certain factors which reappear in every generation, regardless of the methods being used." Gerald Bray

HOW WAS THE BIBLE USED IN THE EARLY CHURCH?

From the earliest days of Christian history, individual Christians and the church at large used the Bible in various ways. We do not know for certain what procedure the earliest churches adopted to include Bible reading as a regular feature of worship. But it is certain that the first and primary use of the Bible was in the church's worship. It is imperative to remember that biblical interpretation was grounded in the church's use and understanding of the sacred text, not in the theoretical analysis of scholars. Following the pattern established in the Jewish synagogue, the exposition of the Word of God was of utmost importance in the church's worship. This pattern started with Jesus' exposition of Isaiah 61 at the beginning of his ministry, which he interpreted in light of his own messianic mission (see Lk 4:16-22), and was continually practiced in the early church's worship (see Ac 13:14-44; 14:1; 17:1; 19:8).

In 1 Timothy 4:13 young Timothy was exhorted to devote attention to the public reading of Scripture. Private study of Scripture was encouraged in 2 Timothy 2:15. The matter of the public reading of Scripture, which was given by the inspiration of God, was able to make the hearer wise unto salvation, which is in Jesus Christ. For this reason, the place of the reading and exposition of Scripture held in public worship was always central. The model Christian service was a Word-of-God service.

The New Testament letters

Also, regard the patience of our Lord as [an opportunity for] salvation, just as our dear brother Paul, according to the wisdom given to him, has written to you. He speaks about these things in all his letters, in which there are some matters that are hard to understand. The untaught and unstable twist them to their own destruction, as they also do with the rest of the Scriptures.

(2 Pt 3:15-16)

were read in the public meeting of the churches (see Col 4:1a; Rv. 1:3). Apparently the apostles expected their letters to be received as authoritative in their own lifetimes (see 2 Th. 2:15; 2 Pt 3:15-16). The letters, as noted before, were gradually accepted, circulated, and read aloud in public gatherings. In this way they became the objects of study and meditation.

The reading of Scripture was accompanied by its exposition. Almost all of the church's interpretation of Scripture and corresponding theologizing developed from the sermon. The real meaning of preaching was set forth by the apostle Paul in 1 Corinthians 1:17-23. Paul claimed that he came to preach the gospel, which he identified as the message of the cross, Christ crucified. This preaching was to demonstrate the Spirit's power so that God's word would be evident to the faith-filled hearers (see 1 Co 2:1-6).

> **And when this letter has been read among you, have it read also in the church of the Laodiceans; and see that you also read the letter from Laodicea. And tell Archippus, "Pay attention to the ministry you have received in the Lord, so that you can accomplish it."**
>
> (Col 4:16-17)

The apostle's theology of preaching was built on the elements of Christ's incarnation, death, burial, resurrection, and ascension. In this sense, preaching in the context of the worshiping community reenacted the event of Christ, the event that provided shape and meaning not only for worship but also for the interpretation of Scripture in the lives of the worshipers.

The preaching of the early church was not a dispassionate recital of historical facts, a sort of nondescript presentation of certain truths, interesting enough but morally neutral. No, the facts were meant to become factors in the lives of worshipers; hence, the constant offer of repentance, pardon, and a place in the kingdom of God.

The church was given the gifts of pastors and teachers so that the community of faith could be built up through reading, preaching, and teaching Holy Scripture to the measure of the stature of Christ in his fullness (see Eph 4:11-16; Col 1:28). The early church heartily emphasized that Christians must be instructed in the Scriptures (see Heb 5:11-14) and that Christian leaders must remain faithful to the tasks of interpreting and expanding the Bible (see Col 4:16-17; 1 Pt 4:10-11). This set the pattern for the church's use of Scripture throughout the ages.

In the early church theological construction was vitally related to, if not inseparable from, biblical interpretation. The basis of all true theology in the history of the church is sound interpretation of Scripture. Most, if not all, theological deviations in the history of the church have been the neglect of biblical truth or the faulty interpretation of biblical texts; thus the importance of careful interpretation. Let's look at how the Bible was interpreted throughout history.

HOW WAS THE BIBLE INTERPRETED IN THE EARLY CHURCH?

The apostolic fathers in the second century found the true understanding of the Bible in the teachings of the apostles. The rise of false teachings, particularly gnosticism, and challenges to accepted orthodoxy created confusion in interpretation. To demonstrate the unity of Scripture and its message, theological frameworks were implemented by such church leaders as Irenaeus (ca. A.D. 140–202) and Tertullian (ca. A.D. 155–212). These frameworks served as guides for faith in the church.

In the second century, the Bible was read with an emphasis on its moral application and function in the Christian's life. But the rise of false teaching caused this functional approach of the apostolic fathers to receive further interpretational development. Beginning with Ignatius and progressing with Justin, Irenaeus, and Tertullian, there developed the contention that if anyone wished to know the true meaning of Scripture, he or she must interpret the texts under the guided authorities of the bishops of the church. All other interpretations were viewed as alienated from the truth and unacceptable in the church.

> **"Above all for Irenaeus, who is defending the main-stream of Christian faith against able enemies, there is one standard of correct interpretation. That standard is the rule of faith as preserved in the churches in apostolic succession."**
>
> Robert Grant

Before Irenaeus, we find the church struggling to define its Scriptures and come to terms with their interpretation. But by the end of the second century a unity of understanding had been reached. The Old Testament Scriptures, primarily through typological interpretation, were understood as an inspired witness to Christ. The work of Irenaeus provided the key for theologically informed interpretation that found its focus in the incarnate Lord.

At times this theological grid forced the biblical text into a set of theological convictions. This led interpreters to decrease the value of the literary or historical context of a passage, but in light of the challenges faced by the church, this theologically shaped approach appeared to be the proper response. This approach resulted in a safeguard for the church's message but reduced the possibility of creativity among the individual interpreters.

Creative biblical interpretation reached new levels with the rise of the school of Alexandria in the third century. Adapting the allegorical interpretation of Philo and the philosophical framework of Platonism, biblical interpretation with Clement (ca. A.D. 150–215) and Origen (A.D. 185–254) moved to a different level. The innovation of Christian allegorical interpretation developed. Allegorical interpretation assumes that the Bible intends to say something more than what its literal wording suggests. It seeks to draw out the deeper, mystical sense beyond the words themselves.

> **"Then [we believe] that the Scriptures were composed by the Spirit of God and that they have not only a meaning that is manifest but also another that is hidden as far as most people are concerned."**
>
> Origen

Clement's work initiated the allegorical method, but Origen was the premier interpreter of this period. Origen, following the threefold makeup of humans, created a three-step interpretive methodology. Yet, primarily he practiced a two-step approach: the literal and spiritual senses. The spiritual sense served an apologetic purpose against the Gnostics and other challengers to the orthodox mainstream, but primarily it served a pastoral purpose to mature the soul.

Origen's genius occasionally led him down wrongheaded paths. But the church's theological tradition, often called "the rule of faith," had a sobering impact on his creativity. Yet it was Origen's total worldview, a blend of scriptural ideas, church tradition, and Platonism, that brought the Alexandrian approach to its new heights, not only in its methodology, but in its spirit.

Because of the christological debates in the fourth and fifth centuries, the followers of Origen became more theologically oriented in their interpretation. The consistent articulation of the church's orthodox faith, coupled with pastoral concerns for the edification of the faithful, provided parameters and norms for the implementation of allegorical practices. Allegorical interpretation tended to give way to analogical interpretation. The successors of Origen were challenged by the school of Antioch with its emphasis on a literal and historical interpretation.

The great Antiochene interpreters included John Chrysostom (ca. A.D. 347–707) and Theodore of Mopsuestia (ca. A.D. 350–428). Like the Alexandrians, the Antiochene fathers brought certain traditions and philosophical presuppositions to the biblical text. Yet, the Antiochenes' philosophical foundation was more Aristotelian than Platonic. The mature interpretation of Theodore

> **"It was this question of history which most disturbed Theodore [of Mopsuestia] , because he recognized that an allegorical treatment of Adam, for example, would undermine the claim of Christ to be the new Adam. If the fall of humankind were merely a fable, how could redemption have any real meaning?"**
>
> Gerald Bray

and Chrysostom, while literal, was not a crude or wooden literalism that failed to recognize figures of speech in the biblical text. They thought of biblical inspiration as a divinely given quickening of the writers' awareness and understanding, in which their individuality was not impaired and their intellectual activity remained under conscious control.

The Antiochenes focused on the biblical writers' aims, motivations, usages, and methods. They believed that the literal-historical sense of Scripture was primary and from it moral applications were to be made. In continuity with the previous practices of Jesus and the apostles, the Antiochenes read Scripture christologically through the use of typological methods.

The Alexandrians' allegorical interpretations tended to lead the soul into a realm of true knowledge where the vision of truth could be discovered. On the other hand the Antiochene interpreters sought to lead people into a truly moral life that developed in goodness and maturity that would continue into eternity.

> **"The first thing one notices is that Augustine has squeezed some 9,000 words of commentary from a text that runs (in his version) a mere seventeen words. He is not always so prolix, of course, but Augustine finds a great deal in his chosen texts—partly because, being thoroughly convinced of their divine authority, he expects to find a great deal in them."**
>
> Thomas Williams

As the church moved into the fifth century, an eclectic and multi-faceted approach to interpretation developed, which sometimes emphasized the literal and historical and sometimes the allegorical but always the theological. Augustine (A.D. 354–430) and Jerome (ca. A.D. 341–420) established the directions for this period. The biblical text was interpreted in its larger context, understood as the biblical canon. The biblical canon established parameters for validating both typological and allegorical interpretations so that the historical meaning remained primary, even though the deeper spiritual meaning was not ignored. Neither the allegorical practices of Alexandria nor the historical emphases of Antioch dominated. A balanced and multifaceted interpretation emerged that influenced practices in the Middle Ages as in Reformation times. This balanced approach to interpretation was influenced by (1) pastoral and theological concerns, (2) presuppositions that viewed the text from the standpoint of faith, and (3) interpretations that produced edification among the saints, love toward neighbor, benefit and blessing for the church, and primarily a knowledge of and love for God.

HOW WAS THE BIBLE INTERPRETED IN THE MIDDLE AGES?

From the time of Augustine, the church, following the lead of John Cassian (d. ca. 433), subscribed to a theory of the fourfold sense of Scripture. The literal sense of Scripture could and usually did nurture the virtues of faith, hope, and love, but when it did not, the interpreter could appeal to three additional virtues, each sense corresponding to one of the virtues. The allegorical sense referred to the church and its faith—what it should believe. The tropological sense referred to individuals and what they should do—corresponding to love. The anagogical sense pointed to the church's future expectation—corresponding to hope.

Bernard of Clairvaux (1090–1153), in the twelfth century, clearly explicated and practiced this fourfold approach. In the fourteenth century Nicholas of Lyra (1265–1349) summarized this medieval theory in a much quoted rhyme:

Littera qesta docet (The letter teaches facts),
Quid credas allegoria (Allegory what one should believe),
Moralis quid agas (Tropology what one should do),
Quo tendas anagogia (Anagogy where one should aspire).

For example, the city of Jerusalem, in all of its appearances in Scripture, was understood literally as a Jewish city, allegorically as the Church of Christ, tropologically as the souls of women and men, and anagogically as the heavenly city.

Thomas Aquinas (1224–1274) wanted to establish the spiritual sense more securely in the literal sense than had been the case in earlier medieval thought. He returned to the Augustinian patterns but because of his Aristotelian emphases he maintained that the literal sense of Scripture has to do with the sign-character of words, and the spiritual sense with the sign-character of things. Thus, he was able to demonstrate that the spiritual sense of Scripture was always based on the literal sense and derived from it. Thomas also equated the literal sense with the meaning of the text intended by the author. The medieval interpreters admitted that the words of Scripture contained a meaning in the historical situation in which they were first uttered, but overall these medieval theologians denied that the final and full meaning of those words was restricted to what the first audience thought or heard.

> **"...all the senses [of Scripture] are founded on one—the literal —from which alone can any argument be drawn, and not from those intended in allegory...."**
>
> Thomas Aquinas, *Summa Theologica*

HOW WAS THE BIBLE INTERPRETED BY THE REFORMERS?

Martin Luther (1483–1546), the Great Reformer, started his career as a biblical interpreter by employing the allegorical method but later abandoned it. Yet it was Desiderius Erasmus (1466–1536) more so than Luther, who through the influence of John Colet (1466–1519) rediscovered the priority of the literal sense. Erasmus must always hold a cherished position among interpreters of Holy Scripture. He exemplified the finest in Renaissance scholarship that emphasized the original sources. The ultimate source to which he returned was the Greek New Testament. Erasmus possessed a truly historical understanding of ancient texts, but he also desired that the texts bring edification to the readers through the spiritual sense as well.

As significant and innovative as Erasmus' works were, the pivotal figures in biblical studies during the Reformation period were Martin Luther and John Calvin (1506–1564). Calvin was the finest interpreter of the Reformation. He developed the grammatical-historical method of interpretation as revised by Erasmus, focusing the place of meaning in the historical interpretation and developing the spiritual message directly from the text. In his commentary on Romans, he inscribed a dedication that read:

> *Since it is almost the interpreter's only task to unfold the mind of the writer he has undertaken to expound, he misses his mark, or at least strays outside his limits, by the extent to which he leads his readers away from the meaning of his author . . . It is presumptuous and almost blasphemous to turn the meaning of Scripture around without due care, as though it were some game that we were playing. And yet many scholars have done this at one time.*

While Erasmus and Luther broke tradition to establish a new Protestant approach to interpretation, Calvin exemplified it with his touch of genius. Where Luther was bold, sweeping, and prophetic, Calvin was more scholarly and painstaking. Luther was a prophet, a preacher; Calvin, a scholarly lecturer. Indeed in the eyes of some, he is regarded as the greatest interpreter in the history of the Christian church.

Yet, it was Martin Luther, through the use of his christological method of interpretation, who broke the stronghold of allegorical interpretation. From his commitment to *sola scriptura*, Luther felt he must stress first of all that the historical sense is the true sense and only sense that provides a framework for sound doctrine. In rejecting allegorical interpretation, Luther said, "When I was a monk, I allegorized everything. But after lecturing on the epistle to the Romans, I came to have some knowledge of Christ. For therein I saw that Christ is not an allegory, and I learned to know what Christ actually was" (*Luther's Works*, ed. J. Pelikan [St. Louis: Concordia, 1955], 42:173).

> **"There is not on earth a book more lucidly written than the Holy Scripture."**
>
> Martin Luther

Luther also insisted that the Bible itself is its own best interpreter. In this principle he followed the great Augustine. He maintained that the true principles of biblical interpretation are to be developed from the biblical sources.

Underlying these commitments was a complete trust in the Bible's truthfulness and authority. Luther believed that Scripture is to be understood above all human thinking—for it is the Word of God itself. Believing that the God of truth had spoken in Scripture, Luther believed that humans must stand under Scripture's authority.

Luther contended that reason can be used to understand truth, but it can not be used to judge the truth value of Scripture. However, Luther's practice did not often match his theory. He did not accept Esther, James, and Jude as canonical. Even with these inconsistencies, Luther maintained that theology has to be brought in line with the Bible rather than the other way around.

Luther wrote important commentaries on Romans and Galatians. He failed as mentioned above to find equal value in all the writings of Scripture, judging those that most clearly conveyed the biblical gospel to be superior. He observed:

> In short, St. John's Gospel and his first Epistle; St. Paul's Epistles, especially those to the Romans, Galatians and Ephesians; and St. Peter's first Epistle—these are the books which show you Christ and teach everything which is necessary

and blessed for you to know, even if you never see or hear any other book or teaching. Therefore in comparison with them, St. James's Epistle is a right strawy epistle, for it has no evangelical quality about it (*Luther Works*, 35:361–62).

Luther's bold advance over the fourfold allegorical methodology of the Middle Ages paved the way for the Reformation. However, it was John Calvin who, in a sense, "out Luthered" Luther to develop a wholistic model of biblical interpretation for the Reformation.

> "In Calvin we find a balance between the text, its meaning and its application which has seldom if ever been equaled in the life of the church."
>
> Gerald Bray

John Calvin wrote commentaries on every book in the New Testament except Revelation and 2 and 3 John. His works evidenced and applied theological interpretation. Always insisting that Scripture interprets Scripture, Calvin rejected allegorical interpretation and emphasized the necessity of examining the historical and literary contexts while comparing Scriptures that treated common subjects.

Calvin, more consistently than Luther or others who preceded him, developed an inductive and literal approach to interpretation. His adherence to the supremacy of Scripture made him less free with his criticism of Scripture. Calvin attempted to synthesize James and Paul rather than reject one or the other. His sound method of harmonization still can serve the church in a healthy way.

Though Calvin was undeniably committed to the absolute truthfulness of Scripture, he was not driven to harmonize every tension or potential problem. If he had no solution, he simply let a problem stand rather than give an artificial solution or question Scripture's authority. Above all, Calvin appealed to the witness of the Holy Spirit as a guide for understanding and interpreting Scripture. He maintained that the testimony of the Holy Spirit is more important than all reason. It is the inward testimony of the Spirit that binds the Scriptures upon a person's heart and conscience. Calvin maintained that the same Spirit who inspired the biblical writings must also work in the hearts and minds of interpreters to persuade them of the meaning and authority of the Bible. He consistently appealed to the illumination of the Spirit above human judgment so as to affirm the full authority of the Bible. Thus Calvin, like Luther, believed that the Bible ultimately must be interpreted, applied, and experienced in order to be truly and redemptively understood. Their emphasis on the christological meaning of Scripture linked the reformers with Jesus, the apostles, and the early church.

HOW HAS THE BIBLE BEEN INTERPRETED SINCE THE REFORMATION?

It is commonly believed that the followers of the Reformers shrank from the freedom in interpretation employed by Luther. While this is an overstatement and an oversimplification, it is true that they conducted their exposition along new theological boundaries, establishing a new protestant scholasticism. This new form of scholasticism resulted in an authoritative and dogmatic interpretation. Almost simultaneously, enlightenment thought began to develop. This movement rejected both authoritative and dogmatic approaches, resulting in two reactions: (1) the newfound pietism of Philipp Jakob Spener (1635–1705) and of August Herman Franke (1663–1727) and (2) the historical-critical method that stressed the importance of the historical over the theological interpretation of the Bible, pioneered by Johann Semler (1725–1791) and Johann David Michaelis (1717–1791).

These different models are still

> **"Pietism broke the grasp of confessional orthodoxy, but it raised up no theological leaders to take the place of the older dogmatic theologians. The critical, rationalist spirit of the eighteenth century...invaded Germany and found the intellectual field largely barren."**
>
> Robert Handy

present as we prepare to enter the 21st century. The functional/pietistic approach is common among all who read the Bible devotionally but are not really concerned with historical, grammatical or theological matters. Rather the stress in this approach is on practical application and moral response. Reformation emphases attempt to interpret Scripture in a confessional manner consistent with the insistence on the supremacy and truthfulness of the Bible. The strengths of this approach are its attempts to understand Scripture in its historical context, its commitment to faith presuppositions, and the establishment of theological parameters to guard against what the church perceives as heresy. The historical-critical model, though prone to skeptical and wrongheaded readings of the biblical text, nevertheless encourages creativity, as well as serious intellectual and academic pursuits in the realm of biblical interpretation. In our next chapter we will seek to develop a fruitful model of biblical interpretation built on the strengths of the various approaches developed throughout the history of the church. Learning from the strengths of the past and seeking to avoid the pitfalls of those who have erred in previous days, we will seek to develop a working model for faithful Christ-followers.

CHAPTER TWO KEY DEFINITIONS

ALEXANDRIAN SCHOOL: Alexandria was a center of great learning. Here Philo developed his allegorical hermeneutics. The school of thought represented in Alexandria had streams of Platonic, neo-Platonic, and Gnostic thought, and these streams of thought influenced the way Judaism and Christianity were articulated. At the beginning of the third century A.D. Alexandria became important as a seat of Christian theology. The school was characterized by its dependence upon neo-Platonic philosophy and its application of the allegorical method of biblical interpretation.

ALLEGORICAL INTERPRETATION: That kind of interpretation which assumes that the text to be interpreted says or intends to say something other than what its literal wording suggests. It seeks to draw out a deeper, mystical sense not derivable from the words themselves.

ANAGOGICAL INTERPRETATION: A method of biblical interpretation that seeks to unfold the spiritual meaning of a Scripture passage as it relates to eternal or future realities.

ANTIOCHENE SCHOOL: The school of biblical interpretation and theology popular from the third to the eighth centuries A.D. that developed in Antioch of Syria. The approach focused on the literal and historical in contrast to that which previously had developed in Alexandria. Interpreters who followed this approach seemed to be dependent on Aristotle and that philosophical tradition.

APOSTOLIC FATHERS: A group of early Christian writers believed to have had direct contact with the apostles of the early church. The term was used to describe the earliest noncanonical writings of the late first and second centuries.

AUTHORITATIVE HERMENEUTICS: A way of interpreting Scripture to point out the false beliefs of heretics. This was accomplished by establishing the correct theological meaning of the Scripture by the authority of the bishop or the "rule of faith" (the *regula fides*).

CHRISTOLOGICAL INTERPRETATION: The Greek word *Christus* means "annointed one" and is the equivalent of the Hebrew *Mashiah* (Messiah). Christological interpretation reads the Old Testament in light of the belief that Jesus of Nazareth is the Messiah/Christ and the fulfillment of the Old Testament promises and prophesies.

HERMENEUTICS: A word that comes from the Greek *hermeneuein*, meaning to express, to explain, to translate, to interpret. Traditionally, hermeneutics refers to a theory of interpretation, that which seeks to establish the principles, methods, and rules needed in the interpretation of written texts, particularly sacred texts.

HISTORICAL-CRITICAL METHOD: A term used broadly to describe all methodologies related to the study of biblical texts. It emphasizes historical, philological, and archaeological analysis of biblical texts to discover the historical settings of a document, such as the times, place, and sources behind the text.

SENSUS PLENIOR: A Latin term indicating that God intended a fuller meaning for a passage of Scripture, although it was not clearly understood by the human author or the original hearers/readers.

CHAPTER THREE
INTERPRETING
THE BIBLE

We have to admit that neither one of us is a golfer. If fact—let's just be up front about it—we hate golf! Every time we have played golf we have thought of all the books, or in George's case the blueberry bushes, that money could have bought. We know others who love the game and play it well; the gifts of God are various! However, we have never given the time and effort to really learn the game. Even so, if someone were willing to pay us enough, we could play eighteen holes of golf and live through it (others on the course at the time might not). Our approach to the ball would be awkward, our swings inconsistent and balky, and our strategies undeveloped. In addition, it would be possible to use drivers for putting, putters for driving, and wedges for long shots down the fairway. Yet, these "methods" would be neither effective nor efficient. In golf, method may not be everything, but it is very, very important. So, although we would finally get from the first tee to the eighteenth green, it would not be a pretty round of golf. In fact, there would be trips out of bounds, in the rough, and in search of lost balls. If past experience is any indicator, the experience would be quite frustrating and unfulfilling. Without a well-developed method, or with a faulty use of "the tools of the trade," the game cannot be played well and efficiently. The same can be said for study of the Bible.

The goal of this chapter is to set forth a methodology for reading and studying God's Word in preparation for teaching and preaching in our contemporary culture. As demonstrated by our history of biblical interpretation in chapter two, from the earliest days of Christian history Christians have used the Bible in various ways. This rich heritage continues to influence today's Christians as they study, interpret, teach, and preach the Bible.

PRIOR COMMITMENTS NEEDED FOR BIBLICAL INTERPRETATION

KEY PRESUPPOSITIONS

1. **Ultimately, God is the author of the Bible.**

2. **God seeks to build long-term relationship through these writings.**

3. **Jesus Christ is the key to understanding the Bible.**

First, we must commit to **identifying our own presuppositions**, since all understanding requires a framework or context in which to exist. *No one approaches the Bible without presuppositions.*

A key presupposition is that the Bible is God's Word. The books of the Bible were written by a variety of human authors over a long period of time, but God is ultimately the author of those books. Interpreting the Bible as God's Word will yield far different results than reading it as a collection of merely human documents. If you're like me, you get lots of junk mail. Let's suppose that in your mailbox one day, along with a number of pieces of junk mail, you pull out an envelope of fine vellum. You notice that the address is not mass-produced but has been handwritten. You notice further that the return address, also handwritten, says 1600 Pennsylvania Avenue, Washington, D.C. Your entire mindset changes. You won't quickly discard this envelope without opening it. You won't even rip into it carelessly. Rather you will carefully open the envelope and read slowly this personal note from the president of the United States. How much more carefully will we approach a document that has as its Author the Living God!

A second key presupposition is that the purpose of the Bible is for God to build a relationship with us. This is not just information to fill our minds. This Person who created the universe seeks to be our friend. Going back to our illustration of the envelope from the White House, if we see that the president is just asking for our vote or for a campaign contribution, our mind will be shaped in one direction. We may or may not comply. But if the tone of the letter is that the president is seeking a long-term friendship with us and that this is one of many letters we can expect from the president, our attitude will be quite different as we finish this letter and read others.

A third presupposition is that the Bible should be interpreted in light of the centrality of Jesus Christ and for the good of the church. Therefore, the Bible should be seen as "Christo-centric," the Old Testament canon foreshadowing and foretelling the coming of Christ, and the New Testament bearing witness to and explaining the implications of the Messiah's first coming.

In more specific matters of interpretation, as we approach certain texts, especially those that have been interpreted variously in the history of the church, we should attempt to bracket our own prior understanding of those texts and be teachable. For example, concerning issues like specific interpretations of eschatology, or the exact nature of the relationship between God's sovereignty and human responsibility, the church has had vigorous dialogue through the centuries. These issues, however, while very important, have not been considered the core doctrines of the faith. Therefore, we should attempt to be ruthlessly honest in our study of particular texts as we encounter such issues and must reject the temptation to read our theological frameworks into the text.

A second commitment, therefore, is **the willingness to submit to the text and obey what it says**. Thus, we come to the text as authentic learners, not as those who simply would co-op the text of Scripture for their own ends. Therefore, the ultimate goal of scriptural study is to apply the text to life. Thus, a broad understanding of interpretation cannot be limited to the grammatical-historical techniques that help the interpreter understand the original meaning of the text. For those who rightly accept the Bible as an inspired sacred text, the church's book, the record of God's unique self-revelation, its interpretation must lead to questions concerning the demands of the text on one's life and community. The grammatical-historical level is foundational and fundamental, but there are the levels of theological reflection and application that cannot be ignored. The grammatical-historical level can help us determine the primary, historical meaning of the Bible, but the theological interpretation helps us see how the text under consideration fits into the whole of God's revelation. Further, application then demands that we discern the specific ways God's revealed truth calls for obedience and submission in both personal and corporate life.

A third commitment involves **our reliance upon the illuminating work of the Holy Spirit**. It is through the ministry of the Holy Spirit that God provides the resource for such obedient understanding of his truth. The illuminating work of the Holy Spirit does not dispense with hard work and solid principles of interpretation. It does mean that the Holy Spirit brings the text alive so that it can be properly understood and applied to our lives individually, as well as to the life of the church.

This latter aspect must not be ignored when we teach or preach the Bible in our contemporary setting. As interpreters of the biblical text, we must constantly be aware of the temptation of individualism. We need to recognize our participation in the body of Christ and do our work as interpreters for the good of others in the community of faith. The church is the instrument that the Spirit uses to provide accountability for our interpretation and to guard against wrongheaded and individualistic approaches to the text. It provides a check against self-serving conclusions that may be limited by our own circumstances. We also recognize that the Church of Jesus Christ is a worldwide fellowship that crosses cultural boundaries.

> **"It is a piece of modern arrogance held by liberal and fundamentalist alike, to suppose that one's own reason and experience can search out the Scriptures afresh and discover the real meaning of faith and revelation, apart from the guiding light of the 'cloud of witnesses.'"**
>
> Michael Horton

This means that interpretation must make sense to others in Christ's worldwide body, as well as to those in our local setting.

STEPS FOR INTERPRETING THE BIBLE FOR TEACHING AND PREACHING

We now work our way through seven steps constituting a model for study, interpretation, application, and proclamation. With each step we will explain the aim of that step, indicate the tools needed, and provide examples from the Scripture for your consideration. The last two steps, application and proclamation, will be expanded in the final two chapters of this book. It is important that you process these steps as we work our way through them. Therefore, we suggest that you take a pen and write down insights as we work our way through these steps, as if you were doing a Bible study.

But first, let us give a general framework for our approach, which may be described as a "historical-grammatical" method to inductive Bible study. Preeminently in this approach, it is vital to interpret Scripture in light of the historical and cultural backgrounds of the time; God's Word must be allowed to say first what it was saying to the readers and hearers of that time, rather than what we think it should have said, or what we think it is saying to us today. In this way we respect God's choice of place, time, and circumstance in which he inspired Scripture. In other words, we must ground our interpretations of Scripture in the original, intended meanings of the text and then must ground theological reflection, and the resulting application and communication, in sound interpretation.

The primary study goal of interpreters, therefore, is historical, in the sense that we are endeavoring to discover what the biblical texts meant to their authors in their relationships with their readers. Our approach calls for a grammatical (i.e., an understanding of the words and relationships between words in their literary contexts) and historical (i.e., grounded in the historical contexts) interpretation that attempts to grasp the meaning an author intended to convey in what was written. Interpreters, then, cannot understand what the biblical writers meant except by what they have actually written.

Once we have established as best we can the author's intended meanings, then we can probe the significance of the text for us today, and it is vital to make this distinction between "meaning" and "significance." "Meaning" is what the biblical author intended when addressing the original readers. The "significance" of the biblical text includes all the various ways a text can be applied in line with the author's intended meaning.

> "We have no access to the mind of Jeremiah or Paul except through their recorded words. *A fortiori*, we have no access to the word of God in the Bible except through the words and the minds of those who claimed to speak in his name. We may disbelieve them, that is our right; but if we try, without evidence, to penetrate to a meaning more ultimate than the one the writers intended, that is our meaning, not theirs or God's."
>
> G.B. Caird

1. *What did the text mean initially?*
2. *What is the significance of that today?*

Therefore, a good model of interpretation should move from the discernment of the meaning of the text, within its historical and literary contexts, to that text's significance for today. Thus our seven steps of Bible study move from our choice of a text to study, through steps that aid in discerning the text's meanings for the original audience, all the way to the application and proclamation of the text today (see chart on page 48).

STEP 1. CHOOSE A TEXT AND PREPARE SPIRITUALLY

For the sake of our discussion, we are going to study Philippians 2:5-11 as our primary example in the following pages. Record your observations in the work section on the opposite page. As we work our way through the seven steps of Bible study we will also address

Choose a Text and Prepare Spiritually	Study the Backdrop for the Text	Work on Translations and General Observation	Perform Word and Concept analysis	Study the Broader Biblical and Theological Contexts	Apply the Text	Proclaim Its Truths
Step 1- Ask: What is the text on which I will focus?	Step 2-Ask: What is the ceneral historical situation of the book?	Step 3-Do: A basic translation of the text (if you have the language skills), or compare 4-5 good translations.	Step 4-Do: Identify key terms or concepts in the passage.	Step 5-Do: Consult the Scripture indices of theologies.	Step 6-Do: Write a thesis statement concerning the main points of the passage.	Step 7-Ask: What main point do I want to get across?
What are my presuppositions as I approach this text?	What, if any, is the immediate historical situation reflected in the text under consideration? For narrative, who are the main characters, what are the locations and the time frames?	Observe key questions concerning grammar and word meanings.	Consult a concordance to see how the terms are used elsewhere by this author and others. Note those uses that seem to parallel your passage.	Read through the various parts of the theologies that deal with your passage under examination	Consider how these principles address the original context, keeping in mind the effect of different genres on the process.	How can I organize my message to communicate most effectively?
Am I submitted to the Lord and dependent on the Spirit as I approach this text?	What is the broader literary context?	Observe key transitions, comparisons, contrasts, and main points.	Consult a lexicon or theological dictionary and identify those meanings that seem to fit the context of your passage.	Write a statement concerning how your passage under consideration fits in a broader theological framework.	Identify parallel situations in our modern context.	What illustrations could help shed light on the key truths I wish to communicate?
Am I ready to apply the truth I find here?	What is the genre (kind of literature)?	Make a provisional outline of the passage.	Commentaries and Special Studies		Make specific application for your own life and those you are to address.	Pray for the filling of the Spirit and the energizing of your spiritual gifts.

Choose the Text and Prepare Spiritually
Philippans 2:5-11

1. Record your initial impressions of Philippians.
From your first reading, does there seem to be a single purpose
to Philippians? Multiple purposes? How does the author
accomplish these purposes?

_____

_____

_____

_____

- -

2. My preconceived ideas about Philippians 2:5-11.

_____

_____

_____

_____

_____

_____

how the steps apply to different types of literature by considering passages of narrative, prophecy, poetry, Jesus' parables, and even other
selections from the epistles. However, following Philippians 2:5-11
all the way through the process will give a clear, cohesive picture of
how these steps contribute to our understanding, application, and
communication of a passage of Scripture.

Your first step is to read the whole book of Philippians. Before you do that, prepare spiritually by praying.

1. Submit yourself to God as you read Philippians.
2. Ask God's Spirit, who inspired this text, to guide you as you seek to understand it.
3. Trust Jesus' promise that the Holy Spirit will guide you into all truth (John 16:13).
4. Express your desire to understand his truth.
5. Express your willingness to allow his truth to shape your understanding, your attitudes, and your actions.

Take a moment right now and read through the whole book of Philippians. It will only take about fifteen minutes. Record your initial impressions in the space provided. Then read through Philippians 2:5-11 again, and ask yourself, "What are my preconceived ideas about this passage?" Perhaps you have heard the passage taught or preached on a number of occasions. Are you ready to take a fresh look at the text in light of the study you are about to do?

STEP 2. STUDY THE BACKDROP FOR THE TEXT

The second step of Bible study involves considering various aspects of the passage's "backdrop." By backdrop we mean the historical and literary contexts in which God inspired this passage. [Insert 2 connects to this] God chose specific times, places, situations, tools, and people through which to communicate the truth through any passage of Scripture you study. As mentioned above, in considering the historical and literary contexts in which the passage was originally crafted, we are respecting God's choice of those contexts and working with those contexts as we try to understanding what the original author was attempting to communicate to his audience.

The Historical Situation

Write out and underline a new heading on your notepad that reads, "Step 2: Backdrop." Under this heading write the subheading, "What is the historical situation of the book?" Here we begin with the historical situation of **the book as a whole,** rather than the specific historical situation addressed in the passage under consideration. There are at least four good places to find the historical situation of any book of the Bible, including Philippians. First, *your study Bible* probably has a brief treatment of the book's background just before the book itself. For example, *The Open Bible* provides about two pages of introductory materials, including information on the historical situation of Philippians. Second, a Bible handbook, like the *Holman Bible Handbook*, published by Broadman & Holman Publishers, or Zondervan Publishing's *Zondervan Handbook to the Bible* can be very helpful in providing general overviews of each book of the Bible. *The Holman Bible Handbook*, for instance, begins its article on Philippians by stating,

> The Letter to the Philippians was written while the apostle Paul was in prison probably from Rome about A.D. 62, though we cannot know for sure. Other possible locations for the writing of the letter could have been Ephesus or Caesarea (sometime between A.D. 54 and 62).

The article goes on to tell about the history of the church at Philippi and the general history of the city. Third, a good Bible dictionary should have an article on every book of the Bible that includes

---

Study the Backdrop for the Text
"What is the historical situation of the book?"

Author:_____

Recipients:_____

Place:_____

Time period:_____

Purpose(s) for writing:_____

---

lots of helpful background information. For example, Michael Martin's article on Philippians in the *Holman Illustrated Bible Dictionary* addresses the authorship, origin, and date of the letter, as does Ralph P. Martin's article in the *New Bible Dictionary* by InterVarsity Press. Finally, any good commentary, such as Frank Thielman's volume on Philippians in the NIV Application Commentary series, will have an extensive introduction to the background of the book.

Take some time now to use one of the tools listed above and write out basic facts on the background behind Philippians. We are just wanting to get a broad sketch here, so do not feel compelled to write out the whole article from a Bible dictionary! Remember, we are just trying to establish the general framework in which the book was written.

When we turn to consider the **immediate historical situation** addressed in a passage we are looking for any aspect of a historical situation indicated by the passage itself or its immediate context. Write out a second subheading under "Step 2: Backdrop" that reads "Immediate Historical Situation." What then do we mean by the immediate situation? In studying the story of Elijah and the prophets of Baal in 1 Kings 18:1-46, for example, the immediate historical situation has to do with Ahab as king of Israel, a time of punishing drought, Elijah the prophet, and the location of Mount Carmel, among other specific historical details. The historical situation of the book as a whole, on the other hand, would have to do with when and why 1 Kings was written and the fact that the book spans from the reign of Solomon down through the death of the wicked King Ahab.

What then of the immediate historical situation indicated by Philippians 2:5-11? The first four verses of chapter two establish the historical situation: The Philippian church was struggling with disunity, among other things. Read those verses and then write out a description of the "struggle with disunity" portrayed there.

The Literary Context

A third aspect of our study of the text's backdrop has to do with the broader literary context, so write out a third subheading under Step

2 that reads, "What is the broader literary context?" By the literary context we mean how our passage under consideration fits into the overall development of the book. For some passages, such as certain psalms and most of the proverbs, the broader literary context is not really a significant factor (although both psalms and proverbs can be grouped according to emphases). Yet, much of the rest of Scripture is either narrative, prophetic material, or letters, and, with each of these, how a passage fits into the development of the book is very important.

The tools listed above under "What is the historical situation of the book?"—a study Bible, a Bible handbook, a Bible dictionary, and the introduction to a commentary—are also great tools for help with the broader literary context, since each should provide an outline of the book. For instance, the *Zondervan Handbook to the Bible* places Philippians 2:5-11 in a section that runs from 1:27 to 2:18 and is titled, "Plea for a United Stand." So the literary context suggested for the passage by that tool has to do with the unity of believers in the church. Tools may differ in how they portray the structure of a book, so read through that section of the biblical book you are studying and discern which approach you think makes the most sense of the book under consideration. Now take whatever tool you have at hand and study its outline of Philippians. How would you describe the broader literary context of Philippians 2:5-11 based on the tool you are using? Write your description on your notepad.

The Literary Context

The kind of literature:_____

Varieties of literature within the whole_____

The Kind of Literature

A final point to consider under the passage's backdrop has to do with "genre," or the kind of literature with which we are dealing. Write "What kind of literature?" as a final subheading under Step 2. Two great books for understanding the different types of literature in the

Bible are *How to Read the Bible for All Its Worth* by Gordon Fee and Douglas Stuart and *Grasping God's Word* by J. Scott Duvall and Daniel Hayes. The kind of literature will determine how we approach the text and what kind of questions we might ask of it. This is true when dealing with literature of any kind, of any era—you need to understand what the author was intending to accomplish by using that type of literature.

If I pick up a novel, I understand that its purpose is not primarily to communicate historical facts but, rather, to entertain with a good story. If, however, I take a book detailing the history of America off the shelf, the purpose lies more in the direction of communicating and interpreting historical facts. Or consider poetry. If I say to my wife, "Roses are red, violets are blue, sugar is sweet, and so are you!" I am not making a scientific statement, commenting on the PH level and "sweetness" of her skin! No, poetry is meant to be figurative and to communicate an emotion. Further, reading a newspaper is approached differently than reading a textbook or a devotional book. Each has its own purpose and "rules of interpretation"; thus they must be read accordingly.

Different parts of the biblical literature also were written using different literary methods and, therefore, were intended to accomplish different purposes. When we consider poetry, narrative, wisdom literature, or the epistles, for example, each has its own "rules of interpretation." *Our goal with each is to understand what God intended to communicate through the human author, but to do so we must understand how the author intended his writing to communicate with his original audience.*

This brings us to certain vital questions we must ask as we seek to interpret the different types of literature in the Bible. For narrative literature, for instance, we want to ask, "What is the significance of this part of the story?" The biblical authors had much material from which to choose, and they chose to include the stories they did for a reason. Psalms and other poetic literature, on the other hand, often communicate emotions expressed in worship. These might include celebration, thanksgiving, sadness (expressed through laments), reflection, or anger (use one of the tools already mentioned to learn about the different types of psalms). Therefore, an important interpretive key when studying a psalm is to ask, "What is the emotion expressed?"

Proverbs, on the other hand, are meant to communicate general guidelines for living. Consider the following passage from Proverbs 4:10-12:

Listen, my son. Accept my words,

and you will live many years.

I am teaching you the way of wisdom;

I am guiding you on straight paths.

When you walk, your steps will not be hindered;

When you run, you will not stumble.

Some may be tempted to take this passage as a "promise," suggesting that an obedient child will be guaranteed to have a long life and will never face impediments in life. Now, there are many wonderful promises from Scripture that are intended to give comfort and hope to God's people (e.g., when Jesus says, "I will not leave you as orphans" in John 14:18). However, neither the human author nor the Divine Author ever intended for proverbs to be promises. This proverb is saying, in effect, that the best way for a child to live is by seeking out wisdom; this is the path of success in life and, generally speaking, will lead to a long and effective life.

"As in the reading of any document, ancient or modern, we must pay careful attention to the literary conventions employed by an author to get the points across. This is particularly true of the Scriptures, for the only authoritative meanings they bear are those the divine and human authors intended in the composition."

Daniel I. Block

Philippians 2:5-11 is part of an epistle, so on your notepad write down "Epistle" under your subheading "What kind of literature?" With an epistle the primary question we want to ask is, "What is the author's main point in this context?" Take a moment now and write out what you think is Paul's main point of Philippians 2:5-11. How does the context govern your understanding of that main point? Be sure to take the book's historical situation into consideration. Also, notice that he starts the passage with, "Have this attitude in yourselves which was also in Christ Jesus" (NASB). What does that phrase tell you about the text's main point?

What is the author's main point in this context?

_____

_____

How does the context give shape to the main point?

_____

_____

STEP 3. WORK ON TRANSLATION(S) AND GENERAL OBSERVATION

If you have ever visited a foreign country in which English is not the predominant language, you know that language barriers can be very real and frustrating. Getting even basic answers to the simplest questions can be a difficult task. Crossing language barriers can also be challenging when dealing with ancient literature. The Bible was written primarily in two ancient languages, the Old Testament in Hebrew and the New Testament in Greek. A few parts of the Old Testament were written in Aramaic. Thankfully, the modern church has a wealth of language resource tools and translations to help. If you have had the opportunity to study Greek and Hebrew, then you know how to use the basic lexicons and grammars to translate the text from the original languages. As always, as you continue through your Bible study on a given passage, you will want to check your translation against modern translations and the commentary given in the best reference tools.

If you have not participated in language study, doing a comparison of modern translations can be a very helpful way to highlight key interpretive issues in a passage. Why? Because translation, by its nature, requires interpretation. With almost any verse of Scripture, translators have to choose, given the context and grammatical constructions, between various possible word meanings. Therefore, the differences reflected in the various translations represent various interpretations of the passage.

Translations tend to fall into three general categories: formal, dynamic equivalence, and paraphrase. A formal translation, such as the King James Version or the New American Standard, attempts to follow as closely as possible the author's ancient message word-for-word. Dynamic Equivalence translations, such as the NIV and the New Living Translation, on the other hand, provide a "thought-for-thought" rendering of the passage, often departing from direct correspondence to individual words in order to give more clearly the author's intended meaning. The final category, the paraphrase, is not really a translation at all, but rather a communication of the sense of the passage creatively constructed from an already existing translation. The Living Bible and Today's English Version would be examples of this last category.

For Bible study we recommend that you stick with the first two types of translation, the formal and the dynamic equivalence. At this point in your study process write, "Step 3: Work on Translations and General Observations" on your sheet. Now choose at least three good translations to compare. You either can work from the copies of the translations you have in hand or write these out on your page in parallel columns. Parallel Bibles, with translations placed in columns side by side, are especially helpful at this point, and there are a number of good ones on the market. For the sake of our discussion, consider Philippians 2:5-11 in three translations: New American Standard, NIV, and New Living (see chart on page 58).

Now, working through the passage verse-by-verse, circle *main* areas of difference between these three translations and, on your Bible study sheet (see page 59), write interpretation questions that come to mind. For instance, notice the different ways the three translations render verse seven. You might write on your sheet, "What is the significance of these different renderings: 'taking the form,' 'taking the nature,' and 'taking the position'?" These questions will be used to fuel further steps of your Bible study.

Are any of these differences the result of variants in the Greek manuscript? You can tell this by consulting the textual footnotes in each of the three translations. Which of the differences will result in substantial differences in interpreting the passage?

General Observation

Also under step three we want to read the passage several times, observing key transitions, comparisons, contrasts, and main points. By observing we mean taking time to look at the passage very closely. Notice the use of key conjunctions such as "and," "for," "therefore," and "because," and ask, "What do these signify?" Take a few moments and work through the passage. Can you identify the main transition within the passage? Write it out on your study sheet under a subheading titled, "Observation." Notice, at the beginning of verse nine in the NASB translation we find the word "therefore." What is the nature of this transition? It shows the result of Jesus' obedience, or stated another way, it points to Jesus' obedience as the "cause" of his exaltation.

What are the key transitions in this passage? These will be marked by words like "therefore," "and," "but," or, "because."

What is the main point of the passage as a whole?

Make a provisional outline of the passage.

What are the major divisions? What are the subdivisions? How far can the subdivisions be divided? What role do the major divisions play in the passage? What role does each of the subdivisions play?

Holman Christian Standard

5 Make your own attitude that of Christ Jesus, 6 who, existing in the form of God, did not consider equality with God as something to be used for His own advantage. 7 Instead He emptied Himself by assuming the form of a slave, taking on the likeness of men. And when He had come as a man in His external form, 8 He humbled Himself by becoming obedient to the point of death--even to death on a cross. 9 For this reason God also highly exalted Him and gave Him the name that is above every name, 10 so that at the name of Jesus every knee should bow-- of those who are in heaven and on earth and under the earth-- 11 and every tongue should confess that Jesus Christ is Lord, to the glory of God the Father.

New International Version

5 Your attitude should be the same as that of Christ Jesus:
6 Who, being in very nature God, did not consider equality with God something to be grasped, 7 but made himself nothing, taking the very nature of a servant, being made in human likeness. 8 And being found in appearance as a man, he humbled himself and became obedient to death--even death on a cross!

9 Therefore God exalted him to the highest place and gave him the name that is above every name, 10 that at the name of Jesus every knee should bow, in heaven and on earth and under the earth, 11 and every tongue confess that Jesus Christ is Lord, to the glory of God the Father.

New Living Translation

5 Your attitude should be the same that Christ Jesus had. 6 Though he was God, he did not demand and cling to his rights as God. 7 He made himself nothing; he took the humble position of a slave and appeared in human form. 8 And in human form he obediently humbled himself even further by dying a criminal's death on a cross. 9 Because of this, God raised him up to the heights of heaven and gave him a name that is above every other name, 10 so that at the name of Jesus every knee will bow, in heaven and on earth and under the earth, 11 and every tongue will confess that Jesus Christ is Lord, to the glory of God the Father.

Step 3. Work on Translation(s) and General Observation

v. 5 _____

_____

_____

v. 6 _____

_____

_____

v. 7 _____

_____

_____

v.8 _____

_____

_____

v. 9 _____

_____

_____

v. 10 _____

_____

_____

v. 11 _____

_____

_____

Now find the primary use of contrast in Philippians 2:5-11. Did you find it? Jesus' status as equal with God the Father is contrasted with his status as a servant. This is stated in the form of a concession (i.e., "although . . ."). The point made is that Jesus' "high" status as equal with God did not prevent him from becoming "low," taking a position as servant.

Provisional Outline

Finally, sketch out a provisional outline of the passage under a subheading by that name. The outline is provisional since we still have a good bit of study to do on the passage. Later we will take all the fruits of our examination of the text and bring them together under a creative teaching outline. However, it is helpful to make a tentative outline at this point to begin to assess the general structure of the passage. Take a few moments and attempt to divide the passage into three or four main points and write the outline on your notepad.

One possible outline might look as follows:

1. A Command (v. 5)
2. A Description of Jesus' Actions (vv. 6-8)
3. The Result of Jesus' Actions (vv. 9-11)

This bare-bones outline is just a beginning but will serve us as we make our way through the following steps.

STEP 4. PERFORM WORD AND CONCEPT ANALYSIS

Words, of course, form the building blocks for any unit of communication. Therefore, when studying the biblical text, we need to have an accurate understanding of the words used in order to understand the passage. Words do not exist in a vacuum, but rather their meanings are determined by the contexts in which they are used. For instance, if I ask you the meaning of the English word "hand," you might confidently indicate the body part attached to your wrist. However, what if I had in mind a "hand" on a ranch, as in "he is a hired hand," or used the word as a synonym of "help," as in "give me a hand"? The term also could be used as a synonym for applause, i.e. "give him a hand, folks". So the word "hand" has no *specific* meaning apart from a given context. Therefore, when studying a word in the biblical text we want to *a) know the possible meanings for that word in the ancient world at the time of the writing, and b) determine, based on the context, which meaning is most likely as used by the author in this instance.*

Word and Concept Analysis

What are the key words and concepts in the passage? Begin with nouns (and phrases like participles that function as nouns) and verbs.

What are the key modifiers of the nouns and verbs? How do these modifiers shape the meaning of the passage?

For Those Who Know Greek and Hebrew

Let's take a word from the Philippians passage as an example: the word translated as "attitude" by all three of our translations. If you have the ability to work with the Greek text, there is a primary tool you should use and two others that can add much to your understanding of a term. In the Greek text the word translated as "attitude" is the second person plural, present active imperative form of the verb *phroneō.* First, look up the term in the third edition of *A Greek-English Lexicon of the New Testament and Other Early Christian Literature,* revised by Frederick W. Danker and based on the older Bauer, Arndt, and Gingrich. (If we were dealing with the Hebrew of the Old Testament, we would use Brown, Driver, and Briggs). The lexicon gives three basic meaning groups for the term under consideration. Philippians 2:5 is the only text listed under the third group titled "to develop an attitude based on careful thought, be minded/disposed." A further translation of the meaning is given as "let the same kind of thinking dominate you as dominated Christ Jesus." You can look in an exhaustive Greek concordance, such as the one by Kohlenberger, Goodrick, and Swanson (Zondervan Publishing), and in some cases this gives helpful examples of how and how often an author uses a given term. However, the lexicon analyzes the various uses of the word for you and, thus, can help you narrow down or identify a meaning in a certain context. Help can be had as well from Balz, Horst, and Gerhard Schneider, eds., *Exegetical Dictionary of the New Testament* (3 vols.; Grand Rapids: Eerdmans, 1990–1993). This is to be preferred over the mammoth work by Gerhard Kittle because the *Exegetical Dictionary of the New Testament* focuses on the semantic range of a word as used in the New Testament itself. Kittle, on the other hand, spans centuries and, while interesting, can lead the student of Scripture in wrong directions linguistically. We are interested in what words meant during the time in which they were used in the New Testament. Beyond these two tools the student of Scripture can consult C. Spicq's three-volume *Theological Lexicon of the New Testament,* which is spotty as to the terms covered but rich in insights from use of terms in the broader first-century world. For the practice of doing word studies be sure to see the excellent little guide by D. A. Carson, *Exegetical Fallacies*, which can keep a student of the Bible away from a host of wrong ways to deal with the text.

For Those Who Do Not Know Greek

There are several good ways to deal with basic word studies for those who have not had the biblical languages. The most sound is to use good commentaries for guidance. For example, Frank Thielman, in his excellent *NIV Application Commentary: Philippians,* says the following about the term translated "attitude" by the NIV:

> The NIV, along with many other translations, is slightly misleading at this point. Its phrase "your attitude" makes Paul's Greek refer to an attitude inside each Philippian believer. Paul says literally, however, "Think this in you," and the words "in you" (*en hymin*) are a common idiom in Greek for "among yourselves." Paul's primary concern, then, is social rather than cerebral: He wants the Philippians to adopt in their mutual relations the same attitude that characterized Jesus (p. 115).

NIV Exhaustive Concordance

Consult a concordance to see how the terms are used elsewhere by this author and others.

ATTITUDE

Eph 4:23	to be made new in the *a* of your minds	4460
Php 2:5	Your *a* should be the same as that	5858
1 Pe 4:1	arm yourselves also with the same *a*	1936

(When you turn to the Greek to English Index Lexicon in the back of the Concordance, here are some of the meanings of *phroneo*. The numbers in parentheses indicate the number of occurrences of that word or the meaning of the word.)

Greek to English Index-Lexicon

5858 *phroneo* (26)
have in mind (2), mind (2) , agree with (1)...attitude (1), being like-minded (1) + 899 + 3836

Thus, using this helpful tool, a person without Greek language ability can gain insight to a term in the text. This approach is the most sound because a trained expert in the language is guiding the reader through a consideration of how the language is used at this point. However, it is best to look at what several scholars might say about a given term, since this will alert you to various interpretations.

A second way to do word study is to use concordances such as Strong's, Young's, or the newer Zondervan *NIV Exhaustive Concordance* by Edward W. Goodrick and John R. Kohlenberger III, which combines the best features of Strong's and Young's. These tools do an exhaustive concordance of a particular English translation (e.g., KJV, RSV, or NIV) and then tag a term either with a reference number that can be looked up in the back for the Greek or Hebrew meanings or with a transliteration of the Greek or Hebrew word. For instance, in Young's concordance we find a reference to the word translated "mind" (RSV) in Philippians 2:5 and the transliteration *phroneō touto*. When this transliteration is looked up in the back we find various possible meanings, including the imperative form plus *touto*, which means "to be like-minded." In the Zondervan *NIV Exhaustive Concordance* the reference to Philippians 2:5 is found under the entry "ATTITUDE," and the researcher is directed to number 5858 in the Greek to English Dictionary and Index. In the dictionary we find various possible uses of the term *phroneō*. These concordances are keyed to different translations, so find one that fits a primary translation you use for Bible study.

A final set of tools that have recently been released constitute a third approach to doing word studies for the non-language student. William D. Mounce has recently published *The NIV English-Greek New Testament: A Reverse Interlinear* (Zondervan Publishers). It is a reverse interlinear because the English translation is on top and the corresponding Greek terms on the line beneath. Thus, the person doing a word study can find the Greek term on the same page with the translation. The Greek words also are parsed or declined and tagged to another tool, *The NIV Theological Dictionary of New Testament Words,* edited by Verlyn D. Verbrugge. Verbrugge's work is an abridgment of the multi-volume *New International Dictionary of New Testament Theology.* For our term under consideration he gives several basic meanings (p. 1311) and then directs us to the broader word group that begins on the same page. In that article we find the following entry:

> Thus, Paul frequently exhorts believers to be of one mind or of the same mind (Rom. 12:16; 15:5; 2 Cor. 13:11; Gal. 5:10; Phil. 2:2; 4:2). Such exhortations, which are linked often with warnings against arrogance, do not spring simply from a pragmatic outlook that puts church unity above all else; rather, they are based on Christ, since he is the one on whom the church is built. This is esp. prominent in the Christ hymn of Phil. 2:6-11 and in 2:5, which introduces this hymn. This verse is best understood as meaning: "Have the same thoughts

among yourselves as you have in your communion with Christ Jesus," rather than simply seeing Jesus' own attitude as a model for us to follow.

This final set of tools is best suited for those who know how to pronounce Greek, since transliterations are not provided in Mounce's volume. However, the tool can be used profitably by those without this ability.

STEP 5. STUDY THE BROADER BIBLICAL AND THEOLOGICAL CONTEXTS

A final step before we turn to application involves placing the passage under consideration in a broader theological framework, so write the heading on your notebook page. Here we want to do three things: consult the Scripture indices in systematic theology books, read through sections in which our passage is used prominently, and then write a summary of how our passage fits in a broader theological framework.

There are a number of good systematic theologies on the market, including those by Millard Erickson and Stanley Grenz. Each has a Scripture index in the back that can be consulted. For example, in Grenz's work *Theology for the Community of God*, we are directed to no fewer than twelve entries for all or part of Philippians 2:5-11. Two of these are offered with reference to 2:5-8 and 2:5-11, for instance, and the reader is referred to pages 635 and 637, part of a broader chapter on "The Ministry of the Community." Grenz uses Philippians 2:5-11 to suggest that a major goal for any Christian community is to give glory to God by humble, obedient service in a God-given vocation. Thus, the passage is used not primarily to speak of Christology at this point but ecclesiology, the purpose for which Paul uses the Christ-hymn that constitutes our passage under consideration.

Once you have read through sections in which your passage of study is used, write out a summary of the broader theological framework in which your passage belongs. In the Bible is it primarily related to some aspect of God's character or nature, to the people of God, or to some other major theological theme? What role does it seem to play in God's revelation of himself, his revelation of truth about humanity, or his revelation of truth about the rest of creation? Such a summary will give a helpful reference point as you turn to application and proclamation.

Scripture Index from *Systematic Theology* by Wayne Grudem

Beginning with this text [Phil. 2:5-7], several theologians in Germany (from about 1860-1880) and in England (from about 1890–1910) advocated a view of the incarnation that had not been advocated before in the history of the church. This new view was called the "kenosis theory," and the overall position it represented was called "kenotic theology." The kenosis theory holds that Christ gave up some of his divine attributes while he was on earth as a man. (The word kenosis is taken from the Greek verb *kenoō*, which generally means "to empty," and is translated "emptied himself" in Phil. 2:7.) According to the theory Christ emptied himself of some of his divine attributes, such as omniscience, omnipresence, and omnipotence, while he was on earth as a man. This was viewed as a voluntary self-limitation on Christ's part, which he carried out in order to fulfill his work of redemption.

But does Philippians 2:7 teach that Christ emptied himself of some of his divine attributes, and does the rest of the New Testament confirm this? The evidence of Scripture points to a negative answer to both questions. We must first realize that no recognized teacher in the first 1,800 years of church history, including those who were native speakers of Greek, thought that "emptied himself" in Philippians 2:7 meant that the Son of God gave up some of his divine attributes. Second, we must recognize that the text does not say that Christ "emptied himself of some powers" or "emptied himself of divine attributes" or anything like that. Third, the text does describe what Jesus did in this "emptying": he did not do it by giving up any of his attributes but rather by "taking the form of a servant," that is, by coming to live as a man, and "being found in human form he humbled himself and became obedient unto death, even death on a cross" (Phil. 2:8). Thus, the context itself interprets this "emptying" as equivalent to "humbling himself" and taking on a lowly status and position. Thus, the NIV, instead of translating the phrase, "He emptied himself," translates it, "but made himself nothing" (Phil. 2:7 NIV). The emptying includes change of role and status, but not essential attributes or nature.

A fourth reason for this interpretation is seen in Paul's purpose in this context. His purpose has been to persuade the Philippians that they should do nothing from selfishness or conceit, but in humility count others "better than yourselves" (Phil. 2:3), and he continues by telling them, "Let each of you look not only to his own interests, but also to the interests of others" (Phil. 2:4). To persuade them to be humble and to put the interests of others first, he then holds up the example of Christ: "Have this mind among yourselves, which is yours in Christ Jesus, who though he was in the form of God, did not count equality with God a thing to be grasped, but emptied himself, taking the form of a servant…" (Phil. 2:5—7).

Now in holding up Christ as an example, he wants the Philippians to imitate Christ. But certainly he is not asking the Philippian Christians to "give up" or "lay aside" any of their essential attributes or abilities! He is not asking them to "give up" their intelligence or strength or skill and become a diminished version of what they were. Rather, he is asking them to put the interests of other first: "Let each of you look not only to his own interests, but also to the interests of others" (Phil. 2:4). And because that is his goal, it fits the context to understand that he is using Christ as the supreme example of one who did just that: he put the interest of others first and was willing to give up some of the privilege and status that was his as God.

TOWARD APPLICATION

As mentioned above, steps six and seven will be dealt with in the final two chapters of the book. However, we cannot overemphasize the importance of building healthy study habits in accordance with the process described above. Rather than a cold drudgery, a heartless discipline to be dreaded, consistent Bible study can be one of the Christian's richest "heart habits." The good work of study serves as the solid, rock-hard foundation for application and proclamation.

We believe that the biblical author's meaning is the objective meaning of the Bible and that the interpreter can determine it through dedicated effort to reach back and read the biblical text in its original context and setting. But because it is a canonical word for the community of believers, the Bible can also be read by and for the present members of the church. It simultaneously affirms the church's confessional parameters, the illuminating work of the Holy Spirit, and the church's belief that all Christians have the responsibility to read and interpret the Bible for themselves. As we commit ourselves to a lifetime of faithful service in interpreting and proclaiming the Word of God, there are several key tools that can be useful for our task. These tools will enable us to be faithful not only with our focus on the historical horizon, but also with our focus on contemporary settings as we seek to live under the authority of God's Word. It is the issue of application to which we will turn our attention following the listing of key tools for faithful study.

HELPFUL TOOLS FOR BIBLICAL INTERPRETATION

General

Bromiley, Geoffrey, ed. *The International Standard Bible Encyclopedia.* Grand Rapids: Eerdmans, 1988.

Brown, Colin, ed. *Dictionary of New Testament Theology.* Grand Rapids: Zondervan, 1978.

Butler, Trent C. ed. *Holman Bible Dictionary.* Nashville: Holman, 1991.

Dockery, David S., ed. *Holman Bible Handbook.* Nashville: Holman, 1992.

————, ed. *Holman Concise Bible Commentary.* Nashville: Holman, 1998.

Elwell, Walter, ed. *Baker Encyclopedia of the Bible.* Grand Rapids: Baker, 1988.

————, ed. *Evangelical Commentary of the Bible.* Grand Rapids: Baker, 1989.

————, ed. *Evangelical Dictionary of Biblical Theology.* Grand Rapids: Baker, 1996.

Fee, Gordon D., and Douglas Stuart. *How to Read the Bible for All Its Worth.* Grand Rapids: Zondervan, 1981.

Green, Joel B., Scott McKnight, and I. Howard Marshall, eds. *Dictionary of Jesus and the Gospels.* Downers Grove: InterVarsity, 1992.

Hawthorne, Gerald, Ralph P. Martin, and Daniel G. Reid, eds. *Dictionary of Paul and His Letters.* Downers Grove: InterVarsity, 1993.

Martin, Ralph P., and Peter Davids, eds. *Dictionary of the Later New Testament and Its Developments.* Downers Grove: InterVarsity, 1997.

VanGemeren, Willem A. *New International Dictionary of Old Testament Theology and Exegesis.* Grand Rapids: Zondervan, 1997.

Bible Commentary Series

Baker Exegetical Commentary (Baker)

Expositor's Bible Commentary (Zondervan)

IVP New Testament Commentary (InterVarsity)

New American Commentary (Broadman & Holman)

NIV Application Commentary (Zondervan)

New International Commentary on the New Testament (Eerdmans)

New International Commentary on the Old Testament (Eerdmans)

New Testament Commentary (Baker)

The Bible Speaks Today (InterVarsity)

CHAPTER FOUR

TYING INTERPRETATION TO LIFE: GUIDELINES FOR APPLICATION

Imagine that you are sitting in the stands of the college football national championship game with seats on the fifty-yard line. The air is brisk, the hotdogs are hot, the fans are cheering wildly, and both sidelines are electrified as the game nears its end. Coaches huddle together, pouring over charts and statistics. Players on the field, sweaty in spite of the cool temperatures, are tired but running on adrenaline, giving all they have on every play. The cheerleaders are hoarse from yelling, and the crowd roars at each gain or loss. Your team is down by three points but has the ball on their own forty-five yard line with forty-two seconds left on the clock. It is third down and five, and you and all those around you rise to your feet to catch every bit of action on the field. When the center snaps the ball the two lines explode into each other. Your quarterback fakes a handoff to the tailback and drops back into the pocket. An opposing linebacker breaks through, but your quarterback fakes a run to the left, sidestepping him just in time, forcing the beefy backer to swing wide and fall to the ground. Suddenly, almost out of nowhere, the tailback has found his way into the left flat, and the quarterback throws the ball to him. Just as the tailback catches the ball an opposing cornerback dives for his legs, but the nimble back deflects the blow, rolls, and speeds down the sideline. Time and again he dodges, ducks, hits, and rolls, avoiding seemingly inevitable tackle after inevitable tackle. Cutting back to mid-field at the twenty-five yard line, the fast back breaks free of the last defender and races at lightning speed for the end zone. You and those around you jump in the air, wave flags, scream "We did it!" (as if your spectator status helped the back along!), and hug total strangers.

Alas, the celebration is short-lived. You see, the back got to the ten yard line and slowed to a stop, laying the ball on the three. Time crawled to a stop. Offensive linemen and defensive backs raced for the ball as the strutting back walked around with arms lifted high in the air in an obvious show of self congratulations. A big burley defensive end knocked one of your team's members out of the way and fell on the ball. The game is over. You lose. Later, when asked why he threw the game, the back responded, "That was one of the most awesome runs of college football history—the run's the thing, man. The run's the thing. They will be showing clips of my run for years to come." You think to yourself, "You bet they will!"

Switch the channel. Imagine that you and your family are invited to a friend's house for dinner. When you walk into the perfectly adorned home, you immediately are hit with a wonderful mix of aromas. Entering the gathering room and kitchen areas, you are struck by the home's pleasant atmosphere and think, "This is going to be an enjoyable evening." Your kids go off to play with their kids, and you and your husband settle in to visit with your friends, as you all gather around the kitchen and chat. You notice perfectly grilled steaks, fresh vegetables from the couple's garden, two fine salads, and—O wow—your favorite dessert, pecan pie! You are so hungry you can hardly stand it. Your mouth is watering. You can't wait to be invited to the table, all the while remaining composed and nonchalant on the outside. Finally, the time comes, and everyone is seated at the table. The host serves water and bread, but to your horror, you notice that the hostess is scraping the steaks into the trash! The host then takes the vegetables to the garbage disposal and throws your pie, your beautiful pie, out the back door to the dog. All smiles, the host and hostess make their way to the table, offer everyone a piece of bread, and have prayer. They notice you and your family are shocked and seem desperate. Shrugging it off, the wife comments, "We just love to cook! In our family we downplay eating, because cooking is the real point! Don't you agree?" You don't agree!

Both illustrations, of course, are comically absurd. Nevertheless they are no more absurd than doing the work of Bible study and interpretation and stopping prior to thinking rigorously about how the text applies to your own life and to the lives of those to whom you are called to minister. Fine study without thoughtful reflection and application is like a fine run that stops short of the goal line or a fine meal that goes in the trash.

As we have tried to make clear in this book thus far, the immediate goal of interpretation is to ascertain the author's intended meaning for his text. Yet, we could say that the ultimate goal of the process of interpretation, within a biblical worldview, is to "hear" the Word of God and seek to be obedient to its call. We must love God with all our minds, and intellectually grasping the truths of the Scriptures through study, is one way we do that—those who are lazy mentally do not give appropriate honor to God. Yet, The Bible makes it clear that we also are to love God with all our hearts, souls, and strength. If we simply stop with understanding the text, failing to apply it to life, we have fallen short of loving God in a well-rounded manner.

In James 2:14-17 James writes, commenting on the second great commandment, the command to love one's neighbor:

What good is it, my brothers, if someone says he has faith, but does not have works? Can his faith save him? If a brother or sister is without clothes and lacks daily food, and one of you says to them, "Go in peace, keep warm, and eat well," but you don't give them what the body needs, what good is it? In the same way faith, if it doesn't have works, is dead by itself.

Faith without works, without application, is dead. James was addressing those who had disconnected belief in the Christian life from active obedience. They thought, "As long as I believe rightly I am OK." James, in effect, says, "Congratulations, the demons have *that* kind of faith!" At times the application may be a right belief, the adjusting of one's understanding to fit what God says is true about some matter. But the movement from understanding the Word to its application in obedience is non-negotiable from the Bible's standpoint. What then are principles that should govern our application of the text?

GET THE ORDER STRAIGHT

Principle One: We must do the work of study and interpretation prior to the work of application. This may seem obvious, but the temptation to rush ahead to some poignant application, that we know our hearer's need, is a real one. Here we have the proverbial "getting the cart before the horse." There are two reasons we must allow good study or reflective reading of the Bible to lay a foundation for application.

First, if the order is reversed, we risk substituting the authority of the text with our own pseudo-authority. In other words, by rushing into what we wish to say about a given matter, we have inadvertently supplanted an authoritative message from God. For example, in Galatians 1:10 Paul writes, "For am I now trying to win the favor of people, or of God? Or am I striving to please people? If I were still trying to please people, I would not be a slave of Christ." Let us say that brother I. Felty Poorly, pastor of Hotpoint Baptist Church, stood to preach on a Sunday evening fresh from a deacons meeting in which things had not gone his way. He wanted the church to pave the parking lot, and the brethren liked rocks. As Brother I. Felty stood to preach, however he was inspired (we won't say by what spirit!). Taking this passage from Paul, the preacher went into a long discourse on why ministers should not give in to the mode of "people pleasing." "Men of God," he told the congregation, "cannot be led by people. They march to a different drummer. To give in on what God has revealed is to forfeit one's status as a slave of Christ." What is wrong with this picture?

Paul's statement in Galatians 1:10 is given in the context of the apostle dealing with a specific heresy. False teachers were teaching another, wrong-headed "gospel" that did not accurately depict the message of salvation. Paul went so far as to say such teachers are cursed (1:8). Paul counters that his gospel is not based on logic or human reasoning but rather on direct revelation from God (1:11-12). Among other things, the problem with Brother I. Felty's tirade is that it has no basis in the passage he used. Galatians 1:10 has nothing to do with an in-church power struggle over a practical, material matter in the life of the church. On the other hand the passage has everything to do with false teaching—especially aberrations of the gospel—and a minister's response to it. If Brother I. Felty had been dealing with deacons who were wanting to admit people for baptism on the basis of social standing rather than on the basis of repentance and faith in Christ, the Galatians passage would have been a good fit. In this case, however, the preacher misinterpreted a text and forced his own interpretation into service in his cause to get the parking lot paved.

Second, and closely related to the first problem, when we move to application before doing the spade work of interpretation, we risk leading others to misdirected applications. Not only did Brother I. Felty attempt to gain authority for his position wrongly by replacing the authoritative message God intended for that passage, but he risked leading others down a wrong path as well. By starting with exclamation rather than proper explanation, the door is left wide open for misunderstanding and misapplication by others. What if a young listener, a teenager, in the congregation took the brother's message to heart but focused on not pleasing people? Being young in the faith, our young teen does not have a broad understanding of Scripture and is not familiar with what the Bible has to say about respect for parents. Consequently, since the pastor's points focus on a person's responsibility to "listen to God alone," the teen twists that message in the direction of her relationship to her parents. If you think this unlikely, you probably have not worked around teens much lately! Our point is that good Bible study and interpretation move both the preacher/teacher and the hearers in the right direction toward what

God intends to be the application of a passage and avoids faulty applications based on pet or personal issues.

LET APPLICATION FLOW
FROM THE TEXT

Principle Two: Get the specific points of application from the passage on which you are focusing. My wife and I have recently moved to a new home. It is an exciting time, and, as a gardener, I have developed a strategy for how I am going to develop my different garden plots. In one area I will have asparagus; in another blueberries, in another raspberries; and in another, my main vegetable garden with tomatoes, squash, beans, onions, and other delights. Right now I am working on preparing beds by solarizing the soil, working in organic matter, and getting the PH level just right. Next spring I will begin planting. I must admit, that I look forward to having blueberries again. At our last home I had set out several plants, and they were just getting big enough to produce a lot of berries. It will take about three years for my bushes to start producing liberally, but it will be worth the wait and effort. Blueberries are fairly easy to grow, and there is nothing like fresh blueberries on cereal in the morning—except maybe raspberries!

One thing is certain. I never will go out to pick blueberries in my backyard and find raspberries on the bush. I will not go to the raspberry bushes and find peaches, or to the apple trees and find grapes. No, the organic nature of each fruit bush, plant, or tree causes it to produce a specific fruit, even specific varieties of each fruit. The makeup of the plant limits what you are going to get from that plant, and it should be the same with application. Our applications should be drawn from the makeup of the individual passages with which we are dealing. How then do we limit our applications, making sure they are in line with the Scriptures?

> "More heresy is preached in application than in Bible exegesis."
>
> Haddon Robinson

Follow these steps:

- Write a summary of the original situation or problem being addressed by the passage.

- Write down the general principles in the passage.

- Note how the principles address the original situation.

- Think of situations in a modern context that parallel the original situation.

- Identify various areas of modern life to which the passage might apply.

- Make applications to your own life and the target audience.

Let us take Hebrews 9:1-10 as an example, and it is a difficult one since part of the author's point is that the system he is depicting, the old covenant sacrificial system, is now defunct. The descriptions here indicate patterns of approaching God, but the point is that those patterns did not win entrance to God's presence for all the people. Take a moment and read that passage.

The original situation with which the author deals is that some among his hearers have become disillusioned with Christianity, probably due to harsh persecution and other social pressures. In their disillusionment some seem to be returning or considering returning to Judaism. What the author seeks to accomplish in Hebrews 9:1-10 is to set up a contrast between the system of approaching God with sacrifices under the old covenant and the new covenant system instituted by Christ's once-for-all sacrifice of himself. These ten verses describe the older system, and, thus, set up the contrast. This is the general situation.

The principles in the passage are not obvious at first glance. It helps to ask, "What does this passage teach me about God, myself, other individuals, non-Christians (and so forth)?" So what are principles in the passage? God has a way he wants to be approached by people. God's way of people approaching him has had to do with covenant relationship (that is, a meaningful agreement between God and his people). To approach God, one must address and dealt with sins. There are ways people have tried to approach God that do not cleanse the conscience. External religious practices may not be effective in approaching God.

How do these principles address the original situation? The hearers of Hebrews were in danger of substituting real relationship with God with an ineffective substitute. God wanted them to have a relationship with him that involved coming into his presence, but they could not come in on their own terms. The choice they were making between the old covenant and the new was a critical choice, and the author shows that the new covenant system progresses from the old covenant system. These worship practices of 9:1-10 are a mere foreshadowing of the ultimate way all the people would enter the very presence of God. Thus, the choice between the old covenant system and the new covenant way of approaching God would radically affect whether the first hearers of Hebrews actually experienced a cleansed conscience and the true presence of God.

What, then, are situations in a modern context that parallel that original situation, and what are areas of modern life to which the passage might apply? People in the modern-day church are bombarded with religious pluralism through almost every branch of media. Moreover, a radical pluralism that holds all faiths are equally valid has become a focal proclamation of some culture-crafters of our day. This is inevitable in a fallen world. The author of Hebrews also lived in a day of rank pluralism. In addition, the pressures faced by Christians of his day, persecution and ostracism, also are faced by many Christians today. Indeed, most Christians, on some level, deal with disillusionment with the faith at one time or another. The passage, therefore, addresses a real felt need in the modern church: How do we deal with disillusionment and the religious options before us? The answer? We grasp the superiority of Jesus Christ as the only one who can win us entrance into the presence of God. If we keep Jesus and his new covenant offering in focus, we can persevere in the faith. To what general areas of life does this truth apply? It applies, for example, to a personal, emotional life of inner struggle with the truth. It applies to a family member who is pressured by other non-Christian family members to reject Christianity and "come back home." It applies to a church being persecuted for its "narrow stance" on the truth of the gospel. It applies to the person who wants to know what it means to have a relationship with God. It applies to these various areas of life and many others.

Finally, in allowing application to flow from the text, we should think of situations occurring in our own lives or the lives of those we address with the truth. When we have specific situations and people in mind, when we can apply the truth powerfully to our own lives, the Bible "comes alive" in a way that truly is life-changing. This brings us to a third principle for application.

Now, take Philippians 2:5-11, the focal passage we studied in chapter three, through the steps to arrive at sound application. You can use either your Bible study notebook or the box below:

Write a summary of the original situation or problem being addressed by the passage.

• Write down the general principles in the passage.

• Note how the principles address the original situation.

• Think of situations in a modern context that parallel the original situation.

• Identify various areas of modern life to which the passage might apply.

• Make applications to your own life and the target audience.

• Identify various areas of modern life to which the passage might apply.

THE INTEGRITY FACTOR

Principle Three: Apply the text to your own life before you attempt to apply it to the lives of others. We might call this the integrity factor, since it takes the danger of hypocrisy seriously and points us to authenticity in our teaching or preaching. In Luke 11:39-40 Jesus blasts the Pharisees of his day, saying, "Now, you Pharisees clean the outside of the cup and dish, but inside you are full of greed and evil. Fools! Didn't he who made the outside make the inside too?" What Jesus declares is that when there is a disconnect between public appearance or profession and private devotion, hypocrisy has raised its ugly head. For those of us who would teach or preach God's Word, we better make sure that we are as committed to the truth of the Scripture in our private lives as we project in our public oratory. Each of us must ask, "Am I living or striving to live the truth of this passage with a whole heart?"

You may have heard about the man who wrote a letter to the IRS. He wrote,

> Dear sirs,
>
> I have not slept well for weeks because I cheated on my last income tax statement. Therefore, please find enclosed a check for $200. If I still cannot sleep, I will send the rest.

That is not the kind of commitment of which we speak! We need to have a pattern of life in which we bring ourselves before the text of God's Word on a regular basis, seeking not only to understand its meaning but also to apply its truth to our lives.

A number of years ago I had the privilege of attending a preaching seminar led by Dr. Stephen Olford. Dr. Olford addressed the various aspects of preparing and delivering a sermon. One point from the seminar stands out in bold relief. This godly man described how, once he has studied the passage to be preached and has crafted his sermon, he gets on his knees and, with the sermon spread out before him, prays through each part of it, seeking to discern if its various truths are real in his own life. I have never forgotten his example. If we are to stand and teach God's Word with authenticity, we must be in a pattern of life by which we are constantly growing, striving to live out the truth. Of course none of us live it perfectly. Nevertheless, God knows our hearts and whether we are taking the Word seriously before attempting to teach it to others.

At about the same time I attended the Olford seminar, this lesson was taught through example in a striking fashion. My pastor at the time was a man much respected in our area for his walk with Christ and his effectiveness in ministry. I remember several people commenting on his integrity and transparency in preaching. One Sunday evening he stood to preach, paused for a moment, then said, "Folks, I cannot preach this passage to you tonight because it is not real in my own life. We are going to have a closing prayer and go home." And that's exactly what happened! This was not a show of false humility—I never heard of him doing that again. His response, rather, was a sincere response from a heart of integrity. He simply did not wish to dishonor Christ by boldly proclaiming that which he had not processed thoroughly in his own life.

BE SPECIFIC

Principle Four: Lead people in making specific applications of the text to life. Notice that we say "lead people" in this stage of dealing with the text. Our job is not to provide all possible scenarios on how the truth of the text might be applied, but rather to help our listeners grow in their ability to think very specifically on how the truths of the text might be put into practice. For this they need specific examples within the framework of specific areas of life, and they need us to model the practice of the Scriptures. Thinking through specifics of how the text might apply takes work, and many are not willing to do it. There is a great temptation to speak and think in vague generalities when we get to the stage of application.

At the end of E. B. White's classic children's story, *Stuart Little*, Stuart, a mouse and the story's title character, meets a repairman for the telephone company. The man is leaning up against a signpost near a fork in the road. One fork leads to the west and the other to the north. Stuart, in his little car, drives up to the man and greets him with a friendly "Good morning," then gets out and sits down beside the worker in the ditch. Having discussed various topics the man asks Stuart which direction he is headed. "North," replies Stuart. The man observes, "A person who is heading north is not making any mistake, in my opinion." "That's the way I look at it," answers Stuart. "I rather expect that from now on I shall be traveling north until the end of my days." "Worse things than that could happen to a person," the repairman responds. He then goes into an eloquent discourse on the value of heading north. He speaks of wonderful places, such as swamps, fields, "orchards so old they have forgotten where the farmhouse is," pastures, "spruce woods on winter nights," freight platforms of railroad junctions, and fresh lakes. There is no specific destination mentioned, but Stuart "felt he was headed in the right direction." The story's ending is wonderfully romantic.

By analogy, some people approach the Christian life in a romanticized, generalized manner, exhibiting a life a spiritual wandering. Rather than looking to specific destinations spiritually, they just head in the general direction of "north." Rather than working on specific areas for growth or specific areas of belief to which one's ideas must be conformed, the generalist thinks in terms of vague, global ideals: "I just want to love people more"; "I need to believe the truth"; "people ought to be more committed"; or "we all need to live as good Christians." There seldom are thoughts such as: "I need to love my

> **"We need to bear in mind that in preaching the object is even more important than the subject. Every sermon aims at definite action. It is meant to make a difference in the lives of its hearers or it is no true sermon."**
>
> William Pierson Merrill

> **"The application should grip and motivate the hearer."**
>
> James Earl Massey

wife by fixing supper tonight"; "I need to grow in my understanding of the Holy Spirit"; "I need to give $100 to the youth missions trip"; or "I need Christ to deliver me from anger towards my boss." Yet, it is when the truth of the Bible is applied in our lives specifically that transformation takes place. As we lead others toward such authenticity, they find Christianity as "real" and "living" because they experience Christ changing their lives in detail, and non-Christians looking in on the Christian community understand that Christianity is more than an empty religion.

In the novel *Les Miserables*, a minister plays host to the main character, Jean Valjean, a man who has been in jail for a petty crime and is down on his luck. Later that evening the thief takes the minister's silver cutlery and steals into the night. The authorities catch him, however, and bring him before the minister for a verdict. He comes at the thief saying, "I am very angry with you," but then says the unexpected. In an act of magnanimous grace, he exclaims, "You forgot the candlesticks!" The thief is dumbfounded. "Why are you doing this?" he asks, as the minister stuffs the candlesticks into his sack. The minister, drawing the ragged man close, looks deeply into his eyes. "Never forget." And Jean Valjean doesn't. The minister has embodied forgiveness. Forgiveness, just a word with so many in the church, just a doctrine from lofty sermons, has now become a living reality to a former thief, because he has seen truth applied at a critical moment. Consequently, Jean Valjean sets his heart to live a life of grace towards others.

Application constitutes far more than a tack-on ending to points of a teaching outline. It involves, rather, integration of the truth into our daily lives and into the daily lives of others. If we lay a good foundation for application with proper interpretation, allow our applications to flow from the specifics of the text, approach application with personal integrity, and seek to apply the truths of Scripture specifically, we will see our study bear fruit in our own lives and the lives of others.

"HE'S PREACHING A VIRTUAL REALITY SERMON. YOU KNOW—THE KIND THAT SEEMS IMPORTANT TILL YOU WALK OUTSIDE THE CHURCH."

CHAPTER FIVE

COMMUNICATING THE RESULTS OF INTERPRETATION

A lady stockbroker had gained millions of dollars for a sheik from the Middle East, and he wanted to give her a gift to show his gratitude. "Please let me buy you a nice house or a car," he pleaded over and over again. Yet, time and again she refused, commenting that she had gotten her reward from doing her job well. Not to be denied, the sheik persisted, and finally the gracious stockbroker gave in, telling the sheik that she had taken up golf recently, and, if he insisted, she would love a nice set of golf clubs. He insisted. Happily the sheik went his way. The stockbroker did not hear from him for several weeks, and she thought that he, after all, had forgotten about the clubs. But one day a note came in the mail. It read, "Dear madam, I want you to know that I am working on buying your golf clubs. I have bought three thus far; two of them have swimming pools."

As this story well illustrates, what we say is not always what people hear us say! Anyone who is married or has teenagers can attest to that fact! Even in the most familiar of contexts, even with the closest of companions, communication has its way of breaking down. How much more difficult, then, is communicating, with a diverse group of modern people, insights gleaned from a text thousands of years old and written half a world away? As we saw in chapter four, we fail the intention for which the Scriptures were written by stopping short of application. So too do we fall short of the mark if we cease our focused efforts with the text prior to considering seriously how to communicate the truths we have uncovered and the application at which we have arrived. The greatest truths, the most relevant applications, must be clearly communicated if we, as teachers and preachers, are to see the process of Bible study and interpretation through to a fruitful conclusion. Good communication is possible, but it takes a lot of work. What we would like to do in this our final chapter is offer several guiding principles for good communication.

THE MAIN THING

First, *always keep the main thing, the main thing*. To this point you have studied the text to determine the author's intent, the author's message. In the last chapter we emphasized that our applications should flow from the text, and correspondingly we suggest that the message as a whole should stay focused on the passage at hand. Too many sermons are what might be called "springboard" sermons—the preacher reads the text and then dives off into whatever topic he wishes, without regard for the passage supposedly under consideration. Such an approach often indicates poor preparation or poor communication skills. The result, however, is it moves our hearers away from the authority of the Bible and, thus, the edification the Bible has to offer. Moreover, it wastes precious time that should be spent on elucidating the text.

One way to keep the main thing the main thing is to write out a thesis statement. In one sentence, write out the main point of the passage and, therefore, the main point you will communicate in your message or lesson. With what main point do you wish people to walk away? For example, I have a sermon on Philippians 2:5-11 titled, "Are You Living Down to Your Potential?" My main thesis of that sermon might read, "Christ provides the ultimate example for right Christian living." In the center section of Philippians Paul gives a series of examples for the Philippians to follow as they were struggling with disunity and false teachers. The first great example he gives is Christ in his incarnation and exaltation. Thus the thesis conveys the main intention of the passage as originally given by Paul.

Above anything else, this is what I want to accomplish through the preaching of this sermon. I want people to take seriously Christ's example as they think about their own lives. *All* of my material in the sermon should serve this main thesis.

BE ORGANIZED

A second principle of good communication involves organization: *organize your material in a clear and memorable way.* I must admit that I am not an organized person by nature. My shop is a perennial reminder of that fact! Often I have started the year with every tool, every piece of material in its proper place, only to have chaos descend as a tornadic monster that jumbles my space I had so carefully arranged. Now, I am getting better at organization, and I have learned to function OK in my shop even when it is disorganized. At times I can remember where the pliers are, or where I put that hammer. Perhaps you think that disorganization merely is another viable style of life (although if we are honest, disorganization can be highly frustrating!). Remember, however, that in preaching or teaching you, in effect, are inviting *others* into "your shop." They are disoriented as it is—they often have no immediate history with this space of yours, since often they have not studied the passage at hand. It is up to you to orient them to the text. This is why organization in a lesson or message is so important. You may wander in the land of ideas and applications and have a general idea of why this passage you are preaching is so important. However, your wandering at best can be a cause for disconnected but stimulating thoughts, and at worst it can be highly frustrating and disillusioning. They have come to hear you say something and, for the life of them, they cannot figure out what exactly you are trying to communicate.

> "Sermon forms are not innocent or neutral. The shape of a sermon is not merely a convenient or logical way to arrange the content; it is an invitation to—perhaps even a demand upon—the hearers to listen to the content according to a particular pattern. As such, form significantly influences what happens to the hearer in and through the sermon."
>
> Thomas Long

90

A passage can be organized in various manners. For instance, the structure of the sermon might parallel exactly the structure of the biblical passage. In my sermon on Philippians 2:5-11 I have three points that follow this pattern. Point one covers vv. 5-7a and has the same title as the sermon: "Are You Living Down to Your Potential?" In this point I talk about Jesus' relinquishing his heavenly position in order to meet a need that only he could meet. "Are You Humbly Living Out Obedience to the Will of God?" is my second point and walks the hearers through vv. 7b-8. The final point reads, "Then You Are Moving Up in Heaven's Eyes," and deals with the balance of the passage. Of course Philippians 2:5-11 deals with the unique exaltation of Jesus, but Paul uses Jesus' pattern as an encouragement to right living that parallels James 4:10 or 1 Peter 5:6. Humility precedes exaltation.

However, there are other ways to organize a sermon. One could arrange a sermon according to key themes in a passage. For example, the latter part of Philippians 2 uses Timothy and Epaphroditus as examples of good Christian ministers. Rather than dealing with Timothy first and then Epaphroditus as Paul does, a sermon could consider the characteristics of honorable leadership found in both of these, God's servants. A sermon also could be

> **"Ernest Hemingway said that his most anguishing hours were spent deciding how to begin a novel. . . . The first three minutes of a sermon determines the effectiveness of the whole message."**
>
> Lloyd John Ogilvie

arranged around a narrative. In other words the preacher can weave the sermon around a biblical story or the story behind a biblical passage. This is most easy, of course, when dealing with narrative passages. The "Good Samaritan" lends itself to story telling. Yet, again using the latter part of Philippians 2, one could tell the story that obviously lies in the background of this passage from an epistle.

Good organization also has to do with how we begin and end a message. A sermon can be launched by reading the passage for consideration then moving to a key illustration that grabs the listeners' attention and moves them to the main thesis of the message. One can begin with a riveting illustration or contemporary event or issue that leads into a reading of the text. Also, one can begin a sermon conversationally and suddenly turn to the main topic for consideration. For example, in the Philippians 2:5-11 sermon I begin by casually talking about my children. If I am the guest speaker at a church and have my son, Joshua, with me, I might start by saying, "Joshua and I are so glad to be with you today. Let me tell you a bit about Joshua." After bragging on my seven-year-old, I suddenly turn to a story from when he was three and used a stencil for an art project. The stencil gave a pattern for him to follow that produced a high-quality picture. This leads into Paul's use of patterns in dealing with the Philippians' problems. A good introduction should get the sermon "off the launch pad," grabbing the hearers' attention and focusing it on the main topic for the day.

> **"Apart from the text, the most vital part of a sermon is its conclusion."**
>
> Andrew Blackwood

The conclusion is just as important. My preaching professor during my college days commented on one student's sermon saying, "You prepared us for steak and fed us hamburgers!" Among other problems, the student failed to land the sermon well, and this is a common problem in preaching. A sermon poorly concluded leaves a vague sense of incompleteness. We have been led through a series of thoughts only to be left wandering aimlessly, wondering what we are to do with what we have heard. A good conclusion might sum up the main points of the sermon or lesson. The climax might come with an especially powerful illustration that drives home the main thesis one final time. The conclusion might give a list of various ideas on practical ways the passage might be applied in the coming week. However the conclusion is crafted, it should bring the listeners to a sense of resolve or closure, and it should do so in line with the main intention of the sermon and, thus, in line with the main point of the passage.

Organization also has to do with how we incorporate illustrations

and applications into the sermon. Do you illustrate every point? Do illustrations come at the beginning or ending of each point? How about applications? Do you wait until the end of the message to give a list of possible applications or do you always have an application at the end of each point? As we will suggest below, using a variety of approaches normally proves effective. The point is, be creative and organized in a way that will communicate with your intended audience. Such organization takes time and thoughtful reflection, but it is rewarded with attentive listeners who benefit from good communication.

TOOLS AND WHAT THEY UNCOVER

In chapter three we discussed numerous tools that make for good Bible study and interpretation, and the importance of acquiring and using such tools cannot be overemphasized. Ironically, pride is one of the occupational hazards that can raise its ugly head out of good preparation in Bible study. Many a young preacher, having discovered the amazing benefits of rigorous Bible study, winds up hurting his effectiveness as a communicator by drawing too much attention to the tools, which should remain in the background. Throughout the message, lexicons, commentaries, and background resources figuratively are pulled from the shelf and hurled into the congregation. As a professor of Greek I have often watched, to my chagrin, a preacher go into elements of Greek grammar or say, "The Greek word here is _____ and is an aorist form" (often the preacher has had just enough Greek to be dangerous!). The statements sound impressive but add no more to the sermon than if the speaker had said, "This word was used variously in the ancient world to mean . . . , and here in context Paul seems to be communicating . . ." The main questions we should ask ourselves are, "Does this statement draw attention to me or does it clarify the passage at hand?" and "Does my pointing to my tools rather than to the text help clarify the text?"

Imagine that you have taken your spouse or a friend to a nice restaurant for supper. The atmosphere is great, the table is adorned, and the smells wafting from the kitchen herald a memorable evening. Yet, when the waiter brings out the food he also brings a mixer, several large knives, measuring spoons, and the trash can. The tools of the restaurant's trade are brought out and displayed side by side with the wonderful meal that has been prepared. Needless to say, the tools would distract from, rather than add to, the meal. A similar dynamic occurs when we do not leave our tools of Bible study in the study.

A related issue has to do with how we handle all the wonderful *information* we have uncovered in our study. I tell my advanced Greek students that, once they have learned to do a thorough job of exegesis on a passage, one of the struggles is knowing what not to say when it comes time to communicate. The temptation is to bring out all those tidbits of cross-referencing, all the delights hidden deeply in our word studies, and all the interesting facts related to the historical background of our passage. Yet, knowing what to share and how to organize what we share is critical.

Back to our illustration of the restaurant: what if instead of the tools, the waiter had brought out numerous packages from the freezer, containers of spices from the cupboards, and bundles of fresh vegetables, all of which were used in some way in the preparation of your meal. The scene would be as ridiculous as that above with a blender sitting in the middle of the table. With any good meal a lot of food—good food—remains in the kitchen. A fine meal draws from the wealth of the kitchen, but is highly selective, and so is good preaching or teaching. Therefore, a third principle of communication is, *know how to focus the message, leaving the tools of study and some fruits of study, in the study.*

ILLUSTRATIONS

A fourth principle is, *make good use of illustrations.* Illustrations as used in preaching and teaching could be described as analogous to light shining through stained-glass windows. All the elements of the stained glass are there, even in the darkest room. What light does is bring out the richness of the stained glass, showing the stained glass for what it is. Illustrations should serve the same function in a sermon or lesson.

"Illustrating may not be the most important aspect of preaching, but it is terribly important."

Stephen Brown

There are some modern homileticians who suggest that broad use of illustrations distracts from the Scriptures, and with *inappropriate* uses of illustrative materials, this certainly is the case. However, when considered in light of the biblical witness, use of illustrations of various sorts may be seen not only as valid but also as a helpful tool for communicating God's Word. Moses, on the doorstep of Canaan, recounted a history of the Israelites and pertinent experiences from their past. The prophets used their object lessons and dramatic enactments. Jesus wielded parables and object lessons as powerful pedagogical tools, and Paul peppered his epistles with figures and examples that supported his messages.

What then constitutes appropriate use of illustrations? The key here is to discern *why* the illustration is being used. Is its purpose to impress or manipulate, or does it genuinely turn a light on the truth of the text in such a way that that truth finds elucidation? Illustrations should never be used to manipulate emotions, although appropriate illustrations can, at times, connect with our emotions. Illustrations should never be forced into service, as in, "Boy, that is a great illustration! How can I make it fit this Sunday?" Finally, illustrations should never overwhelm the passage under consideration. Too many illustrations in a sermon become the lead rather than the supporting actors in the play. Illustrations are used best as tools that support a truth under consideration, making clearer than before.

Not only should we use illustrations appropriately, we also should use various kinds of illustrations. The most often used illustration is the story. A powerful, funny, or interesting story can be an effective tool, helping our listeners connect with the truth we are trying to convey. Object lessons can serve as visual aids that rivet attention on a particular point of the sermon. For instance, last Sunday, following the prophet Amos' example, I used a plumb line to illustrate the concept of righteousness. A plumb line is used in building to determine whether something is straight. When God's standards are placed alongside our lives, are we straight or crooked. On various occasions I have carried books, seeds, tools, and toys into the pulpit. These are objects with which people can identify because they themselves have handled such in the past. Such objects, when used appropriately and effectively, can help them understand the truth being communicated. Contemporary events are another form of illustration. During a national tragedy, such as a school shooting or a devastating tornado, many people in the congregation have been thinking about the tragedy before they come to church. Using current events as stimuli to think about specific truths in the Bible can be effective. Finally, materials from the arts, such as literature, movies, and even works of art, can serve as effective illustrations.

By using various types of illustrations we address truths from God's Word from various angles. Some people learn best by simple presentation of facts. Others, however, learn well through narrative and may remember the point of a passage months later because they remember the story to which it was connected. Still others connect with object lessons because they are quite visual in their learning orientation, and some listeners stay in touch with current events and are grateful for a casting of those events in light of biblical truth.

Good illustrations do not just fall from the sky. They take effort to find and discernment to use properly. Yet, when used appropriately and effectively, illustrations can serve communication of God's Word in powerful ways.

Several years ago, I heard a prominent preacher tell the story of how Winston Churchill, at the end of World War II, called together the leaders of the coal industry in England, appealing to them for an increase in the production of coal. He said that after presenting all the facts, the great diplomat painted a picture for these industry leaders, of a parade at the end of the war. In that parade down Piccadilly Circus would come various branches of the armed forces. Those of the navy would walk by to the cheers of the crowds. Then, perhaps, the Air Force would march by proudly, and the Infantry would parade by to the resounding cheers of thousands. Then, Churchill intoned, at the back of the parade would march 10,000 men with faces blackened by soot. Perhaps someone would yell from the crowd, "Where were you in the hottest days of the conflict?" And with 10,000 voices the coal miners would answer back, "We were deep in the earth with our faces to the coal!"

The preacher then took this story about Churchill and turned it to the church and effectively illustrated the need for common people to be faithful in Christian ministry. He drew a parallel to the end of time and the "parade" that would be brought before the throne of Christ. Various branches of ministry would be marched before the throne, and then finally, millions of common people would be marched by, and, perhaps, someone would shout out, "And where were you in the hottest days of the conflict?" And with millions of voices they would answer back that they were deep in the Word, ministering faithfully for the Lord. Such illustrations can be used to good effect, when they are used wisely and serve as genuine tools to elucidate the point at hand.

THE ROLE OF THE SPIRIT AND THE POSTURE OF COMMUNICATION

Finally, *we should pray for the filling of the Spirit and the energizing of our gifts.* In Ephesians 5:18 Paul writes, "And don' get drunk with wine, which [leads to] reckless actions, but be filled with the Spirit," and in Acts 4:31 we are told that the apostles were filled with the Holy Spirit and started speaking God's Word with boldness. John Stott suggests that the Book of Acts rightly might be titled with the cumbersome but appropriate, *The Continuing Words and Deeds of Jesus by His Spirit Through His Apostles.* Acts sets the pattern, therefore, that the church moves forward by the ministry of the Holy Spirit through committed believers. The work of teaching and preaching God's Word cannot be conceived adequately as a purely human work. The connection of divine truth to human need, the transformation of human lives through proclamation of God's Word comprises a partnership in which we cooperate with the Spirit of God in his work in his Church. Thus the filling of the Spirit involves our yielding ourselves for the Spirit's use in the moment of the preached or taught Word. In that yielding we can also ask the Spirit to energize our gifts so that the Word might be taught clearly and powerfully.

> "When a person is in an holy and lively frame in secret prayer, it will wonderfully supply him with matter and with expressions... [in] preaching."
>
> Jonathan Edwards

As for the posture of communication, we should preach from a posture of humility, oriented to God as the primary audience and the advancement of his kingdom as the primary concern. Any public service can degenerate into putting self forward for inappropriate reasons—and, unfortunately, this often occurs subconsciously. We should check our motives, in other words, and make sure we are preaching or teaching for the right reasons.

BIBLIOGRAPHY

Block, Daniel I. *Judges, Ruth.* The New American Commentary. Nashville: Broadman & Holman, 1999.

Bray, Gerald. *Biblical Interpretation: Past & Present.* Downers Grove, IL: InterVarsity Press, 1996.

Caird, G. B. *The Language and Imagery of the Bible.* Philadelphia: Westminister, 1980.

Carson, D. A. *Exegetical Fallacies.* 2nd ed. Grand Rapids: Baker Books, 1996.

Duduit, Michael. *Handbook of Contemporary Preaching.* Nashville: Broadman & Holman, 1993.

Grant, Robert McQueen, with David Tracy. *A Short History of the Interpretation of the Bible.* 2nd ed., rev. and enl. Philadelphia: Fortress Press, 1964.

Grudem, Wayne. *Systematic Theology.* Grand Rapids: Zondervan, 1995.

Hall, Christopher A. *Reading Scripture with the Church Fathers.* Downers Grove, IL: InterVarsity, 1998.

Lewis, C. S. *God in the Dock.* Grand Rapids: William B. Eerdmans Publishing Company, 1970.

Vanhoozer, Kevin J. *Is There a Meaning in This Text?* Grand Rapids: Zondervan, 1998.

Warren, Rick. *Dynamic Bible Study Methods.* Wheaton, IL: Victor Books, 1981.

Williams, Thomas. "Biblical Interpretation." In *The Cambridge Companion to Augustine.* Edited by Eleanor Stump and Norman Kretzmann. New York: Cambridge University Press, 2001.